A FINAL CHARGE
TO THE CHURCH

PASTOR ADRIAN ROGERS'
LAST WORDS FROM THE PULPIT

FROM THE MESSAGES
ADRIAN ROGERS

A Final Charge to the Church

From the Messages of Adrian Rogers

Published by Love Worth Finding Ministries, Inc.
  Memphis, Tennessee

Copyright © 2024 Love Worth Finding Ministries, Inc. All rights reserved. No part of this publication may be reproduced, stored in a retrieval system, or transmitted in any form by any means, electronic, mechanical, photocopy, recording or otherwise, without the prior permission of the publisher, except as provided by USA copyright law.

Scripture taken from the New King James Version.® Copyright © 1982 by Thomas Nelson. Used by permission. All rights reserved.

Printed in the United States of America
July 2024

CONTENTS

Introduction 1

A Unified Church 4

A Steadfast Church 18

A Spirit-Filled Church 34

A Praying Church 46

A Worshiping Church 60

A Conquering Church 72

A Bible-Believing Church 84

A Caring Church 92

Afterword 107

INTRODUCTION

A FINAL CHARGE TO THE CHURCH

Pastor Adrian Rogers, one of the most recognized and trusted voices of his generation, was known for preaching timeless truths straight from the Word of God. Prior to his retirement, he introduced his final message series with the following words:

> *"I'm beginning a series of messages that I'm going to be preaching, God willing, all this month and next month, that is going to be a distillation of things that I want you to remember—things that I have tried to teach you for more than 32 blessed years."*

The messages were delivered in 2005 to the congregation of Bellevue Baptist Church in Memphis, Tennessee, but the content is as relevant today as it was then and is applicable to all churches seeking to live by the Gospel of Jesus Christ—because, of course, the teaching comes directly from Scripture.

Love Worth Finding, the ministry Pastor Rogers founded to share God's love, is privileged to bring you in this book the content derived directly from transcripts of these messages. Some references applicable only to Pastor Rogers' specific church have been edited so that you, the reader, can digest the material personally and apply it to your own church. Our prayer is that every church, and the Church as a whole, would embrace the characteristics fleshed out in Pastor Rogers' final charge to his church, because these are the characteristics God's Word defines.

May our churches become more unified, steadfast, Spirit-filled, prayerful, worshipful, Bible-centered, and caring. And may we go forward together to conquer new ground for Jesus Christ.

A UNIFIED CHURCH

I want to tell you a story about a man who was shipwrecked. He was on a desert island, and he was there all alone. He had to forage for himself.

Finally, after years, someone came to rescue him.

He had taken care of things pretty well. He had built a nice house, almost a mansion. Next to the house he had constructed a church, and he even put a steeple on top of it. Next to that was another magnificent building.

Those who came to rescue him said, "What is that big place there?"

He said, "That's my house, where I live."

"What is that next door? It looks like a church."

He said, "It is. I built myself a church."

They said, "Well, what is that other building?"

"Oh," he said, "that's another church. I had an argument in the old one and moved my membership."

So many times, the problem is on the inside, is it not?

My prayer for our churches is that we will continue to be a unified Church.

I want you to look at a particular passage of Scripture, where Paul says we are to be "endeavoring to keep the unity of the Spirit in the bond of peace" (Ephesians 4:3). Is that not a beautiful concept? This is the desire of God for His Church: that we have the unity of the Spirit and the bond of peace. The Bible says God hates "one who sows discord among brethren" (Proverbs 6:19b).

> **Behold, how good and how pleasant it is for brethren to dwell together in unity (Psalm 133:1)!**

We do not produce this unity. It is called the unity of the Spirit. But while we do not produce it, we are to preserve it.
This unity is based on three basic concepts.

THE GROUND OF OUR UNITY

The ground of our unity is truth.
There are seven basic truths found in Ephesians 4 that hold up the entire spiritual enterprise of the Church. No one can call himself a Bible-believing Christian who does not believe these seven basic truths, which are the foundation of our unity.

> **There is one body and one Spirit, just as you were called in one hope of your calling; one Lord, one faith, one baptism; one God and Father of all, who is above all, and through all, and in you all (Ephesians 4:4-6).**

Do not let anybody tell you that doctrine does not matter. If our churches cease to hold these great truths, they will lose their unity.

WHAT DO I MEAN BY UNITY?

By unity, I do not mean unison. Unison may be all right if you are in the choir, but not everybody in a church has to sing the same note...that would be boring. We can sing in harmony without singing in unison.

I am not talking about uniformity. We do not have to be congregations of clones. We do not all have to look and dress alike. Uniformity comes from without; unity comes from within.

Even union and unity are not necessarily the same. You can be in the same church and not be in unity. You can take two tom cats, tie their tails together, and hang them over a clothesline—you will have union, but you will not have unity!

So, what do we mean by unity? Unity is doctrinal, and it is spiritual.

Let's think about these seven truths that are foundational to unity. Churches, I want you to get a bulldog grip on these truths.

SEVEN FOUNDATIONS FOR UNITY

ONE BODY

There is one body... (Ephesians 4:4a).

That one body is the Church of our Lord and Savior Jesus Christ.

It does not say "one congregation." The body of Christ is bigger than your home church.

The Church is not a corporation with Jesus as the president; the Church is a body with Jesus as the Head. That is all the difference in the world.

The Church is not one denomination. Somebody asked me, "Are you one of those narrow-minded Baptists who think only

Baptists are going to Heaven?" I am more narrow-minded than that; I think a lot of Baptists are not going to make it. But whether you are a Baptist, Methodist, Presbyterian, Episcopalian, etc., if you have given your heart to Jesus Christ, if you have been twice-born, you are a part of the mystical body of our Lord and Savior Jesus Christ.

There is a local expression of that body. The Bible speaks of the Church here and the Church there, because not only is there that great *universal* Church, but there is also that *local* New Testament body. Every twice-born person ought to be a member of a local New Testament congregation. That is the plan of God.

A man once came to a minister of music and said, "I'd like to sing in your choir."

The minister said, "Are you a member of this church?"

He said, "No, sir."

"Well, what church are you a member of?"

He said, "I'm a member of the invisible church."

The minister said, "I have a suggestion for you: you sing in the invisible choir."

A church is a unified body, *here*, with pastor and deacons and servants, and you need to be a part of that body.

There is one Church. That brings unity. And if you are a dis-unified person, if you sow discord in the Church, one: you dishonor the Head, who is Jesus; two, you wound and mutilate yourself–because we are members of the same body.

ONE SPIRIT

There is one body and one Spirit... (Ephesians 4:4a).

Paul is talking about the Holy Spirit, who is the substance of our life, the secret of our strength, and the source of our unity. The Holy Spirit is the one who binds us together, who tells us we belong one to another.

No Christian knows every other Christian's name. No one does, except God. But we know the one dear Holy Spirit who dwells in each of us, and that is the source of our unity. Sometimes people cannot understand it: how can the Church be so big and yet have a spirit of unity? Because the Holy Spirit that is in me is in you. God's Spirit bears witness with our spirits that we are children of God and that we belong to one another.

I once sat down in an airplane. A man sat down beside me. I made up my mind that I was going to witness to him, so I turned to him and raised the subject of spiritual things.

"Oh," he said. "You're a believer, aren't you?"

I said, "Yes, I am."

He said, "So am I. Mister, I want to tell you something strange: I felt your spirit when I sat down beside you. Something in me said, 'He's one of us. He is a believer.'"

ONE HOPE

There is one body and one Spirit, just as you were called in one hope of your calling... (Ephesians 4:4).

What is that one hope? It is the Second Coming of Jesus Christ.

The Bible refers to "the blessed hope and glorious appearing of our great God and Savior Jesus Christ" (Titus 2:13). All true believers in Christ are waiting for Jesus Christ to come again. You cannot call yourself a Bible-believing Christian if you do not believe in this one hope, the Second Coming of our Lord.

People have different views of the Second Coming of Jesus. They have technical terms—amillennial, premillennial, postmillennial. Some say, "I don't understand those terms." Let me tell you this: you do not have to know the meaning of every detail to be expecting the Lord Jesus to come again. The longer I have been on the trail, the more humble I have gotten about this matter of prophecy. I have moved from the Program Committee to the Welcome Committee. "He who testifies to these things says, 'Surely I am coming quickly.' Amen. Even so, come, Lord Jesus!" (Revelation 22:20).

Matthew 24 speaks about the signs of the end of the age, about earthquakes and calamities. etc. Then Jesus said, "All these are the beginning of sorrows" (Matthew 24:8). The original word used for sorrows is the same word as for birth pangs. When a woman is going to deliver a baby, she has what is called "sorrows," in Matthew 24–labor pains. Without being a sensationalist, I believe we are living in the closing shadows of an age, and our one hope–the only hope of this world–is the Second Coming of our Lord and Savior Jesus Christ.

ONE LORD

> *There is one body and one Spirit, just as you were called in one hope of your calling; one Lord... (Ephesians 4:4-5a).*

We confess one Lord. Who is that one Lord? Jesus Christ. Did you know that the Early Church did not call Him "Jesus" so much as they called Him "the Lord Jesus"? We need to get in the habit of saying the Lord Jesus.

The Lord Jesus has not come to take my side or your side, or your local church's side, against some other church, or anything else.

Jericho was a pagan city. When Joshua came against Jericho, he went out one morning to see what the situation was. While

Joshua was out there, he was aware of a presence behind him. He wheeled around and saw a man with a drawn sword.

Joshua was astounded. He said, "Who are you? Are you for us, or are you for them? Whose side are you on?"

Then the angel with the drawn sword said, "No, but as Commander of the army of the Lord I have now come" (Joshua 5:14a). Do you know what he was saying? *I have not come to take sides. I have come to take over.*

That is what we want: for the one Lord, the captain of the Lord's host, Jesus Christ Himself, to be the Head of His Church. Jesus must always, always, always be the Lord of our dear churches.

ONE FAITH

> **There is one body and one Spirit, just as you were called in one hope of your calling; one Lord, one faith... (Ephesians 4:4-5b).**

What is that one faith? Not *a* faith; *one* faith. Paul is talking about the unified body of truth that we call the Bible. That is also what Jude is talking about:

> **Beloved, while I was very diligent to write to you concerning our common salvation, I found it necessary to write to you exhorting you to contend earnestly for the faith which was once for all delivered to the saints (Jude 1:3).**

There is one faith, and it is God's revealed Word, and we are to "contend earnestly" for it. Christians, get a bulldog grip on the Bible and never let go.

We do not need a new and modern gospel for a new and modern age. If it is new, it is not true. If it is not absolute, it is obsolete. We have the *one faith* of the Church. May our pulpits always have men to stand behind them who will open the Word of God, analyze it, organize it, illustrate it, and apply it. We can have all other kinds of programs, but we must have this one faith.

Just before the dear old Apostle Paul stepped off the scene, he said this: "I have fought the good fight, I have finished the race, I have kept the faith" (2 Timothy 4:7). He was faithful to the faith.

Our churches must never waver.

ONE BAPTISM

> *There is one body and one Spirit, just as you were called in one hope of your calling; one Lord, one faith, one baptism... (Ephesians 4:4-5).*

Is he talking about immersion or sprinkling? No—Paul is talking about something that goes beyond that.

When people give their hearts to the Lord Jesus Christ, they are baptized by the Holy Spirit into the mystical body of Christ. That is, at the moment of your salvation, you are placed into the body of Christ. Remember: the Church is a body, with Christ as the Head. We are the members.

When are you baptized? Before you were ever baptized *in water*, you were baptized *with the Holy Spirit of God* into the body of Christ. "For by one Spirit we were all baptized into one body—whether Jews or Greeks, whether slaves or free—and have all been made to drink into one Spirit" (1 Corinthians 12:13). That is what makes us one.

I believe in water baptism, but that only symbolizes that which takes place when a man or a woman gives his or her heart to Jesus. Sometimes you hear people say, "You've been saved. Now, have you received the baptism of the Holy Ghost?" Friend, if you are saved, you have *already* received the baptism of the Holy Ghost. Nowhere in the New Testament is a believer told to seek the baptism of the Holy Spirit. We are told to be filled with the Spirit. That baptism takes place at the moment of salvation. There may be many "fillings," but there is only one baptism.

ONE GOD

> *There is one body and one Spirit, just as you were called in one hope of your calling; one Lord, one faith, one baptism; one God and Father of all, who is above all, and through all, and in you all (Ephesians 4:4-6).*

We worship one God. His name is Yahweh, Jehovah, and you do not know Him apart from Jesus Christ. "Jesus said to him, 'I am the way, the truth, and the life. No one comes to the Father except through Me'" (John 14:6).

Those are our seven basic, foundational truths, and our unity is in these truths. But here is a second thing I want you to notice: not only the ground of our unity but also the glory of our diversity.

THE GLORY OF OUR DIVERSITY

Did you know that God made us one, and God made us different, all at the same time? Look at the first word of Ephesians 4:7—"But..." Paul is changing direction. He has been talking about our sameness, doctrinally, but then:

> *But to each one of us grace was given according to the measure of Christ's gift (Ephesians 4:7).*

The Greek word for "grace" is *kharis*. This is the word from which we get "charismatic." "But to each one of us [*charisma*] was given according to the measure of the gift of Christ."

God gave you gifts that He did not give me. God gave your pastor gifts that He did not give to you. God gave you gifts that He did not give to your spouse. These are spiritual gifts. God made us different in this Church. So not only do we have our unity, but we also have our diversity. We are not to be a congregation of clones. What we have is unity in diversity.

I am *not* talking about diversity in doctrine. "Now I urge you, brethren, note those who cause divisions and offenses, contrary to the doctrine which you learned, and avoid them" (Romans 16:17). No, there is not room for every kind of belief.

But there is room for people who have different gifts. God gave us different gifts so that He might make us one. Each of us has a grace gift. "To each one of us," Ephesians 4:7a says, "grace was given."

DIFFERENT SPIRITUAL GIFTS

God gave you a gift to serve Him. My heart leaps out of my throat when I think what would happen if every member of the Church were to discover, develop, and deploy his gift. A spiritual gift is not for your ecstasy. It is not a toy; it is a tool. And you do have a spiritual gift. There is a place of service for you in your church.

God gave us gifts that are different, to make us one. Sameness is not unity. In fact, unity comes from diversity. I will give you a perfect illustration: my wife is a woman, and I am a man. We have unity *because* we are different. It is the differences that draw us together. I am glad my wife is not like me. *Viva la différence!*

God makes us different. God gives you a gift, and me a gift, and her a gift, and him a gift, and we do not have to march in lockstep.

DIFFERENT TASTES

One of the difficulties in a church is that we also have different tastes.

Years ago, we had a southern gospel quartet come to sing at our church. I like southern gospel, and these singers were good. I saw people come to this church that night that I had never seen before, and have not seen since.

The next Wednesday night, I asked the congregation, "How many of you like liver and onions?" About a third lifted their hands. "How many of you detest liver and onions?" A third lifted their hands. "How many of you like liver and onions, but only every so often?" Another third lifted their hands.

I said, "Folks, we are hopelessly divided." And over what were we divided? Not Jesus! We were divided over tastes, and those things do not make any difference whatsoever.

I hear people say, "Well, this is my style of worship music." Forget that stuff! We are here to glorify the Lord Jesus. Your next pastor may have different ideas about music than your current pastor does. Then, you will love him, follow him, and believe him.

We are going to be one body in the Lord Jesus Christ. This is the glory of our diversity, and we are to celebrate it. We are to conserve our diversity. We do not all have to sing in unison.

THE GOAL OF OUR MATURITY

Why do we have this unity and this diversity? What is the goal?

> *...Till we all come to the unity of the faith and of the knowledge of the Son of God, to a perfect man, to the measure of the stature of the fullness of Christ...* (Ephesians 4:13).

The word "perfect" means *mature*. Peace comes with unity, diversity, and maturity. Little children squabble and fuss; mature adults learn how to get along with one another. Bickering comes from immaturity. May God preserve our churches from bickering!

GROWING TO THE STATURE OF CHRIST

> **We are to be mature in stature: "to the measure of the stature of the fullness of Christ" (Ephesians 4:13b).**

Do you want to know whether you are spiritually growing up or not? Do not measure yourself by some other member of your church. Measure yourself by Jesus Christ. The measure of a church's ministry is not the size of the buildings, nor the budget, nor the Bible study attendance. *Are you becoming more like Jesus Christ?*

STABLE AND GROUNDED IN TRUTH

> *...That we should no longer be children, tossed to and fro and carried about with every wind of doctrine, by the trickery of men, in the cunning craftiness of deceitful plotting...* (Ephesians 4:14).

Be mature in stability. Get your feet on the rock.

Paul told the Ephesian church, "For I know this, that after my departure savage wolves will come in among you, not sparing the flock" (Acts 20:29).

False cults do not produce converts of their own so much as they try to siphon off Bible believers who do not understand. Because those Christians are not rooted and grounded in the faith, they are drawn away into these false things. They are like little sailboats blown this way and that way "by every wind of doctrine."

Church, get a bulldog grip on the truth. Young people, get a grip on these seven basic principles we have been discussing.

ABLE TO SPEAK THE TRUTH IN LOVE

Be mature in speech.

> ...But, speaking the truth in love, may grow up in all things into Him who is the head–Christ... (Ephesians 4:15).

We are not to speak truthless love, or loveless truth. We are to speak the truth—never stutter, never stammer, never apologize. Speak the truth, but in love. Truth without love is brutality. Love without truth is hypocrisy.

The Bible is a wonderful sword, but it is a poor club. Don't you be a Bible bully, argumentative over the difference between Tweedledum and Tweedledee. Yes, we are never to jettison the truth, but we are to speak the truth *in love*.

SERVING IN HARMONY

Be mature in service.

> **...Grow up in all things into Him who is the head—Christ—from whom the whole body, joined and knit together by what every joint supplies, according to the effective working by which every part does its share, causes growth of the body for the edifying of itself in love. (Ephesians 4:15b-16).**

What is that talking about? Let me give it to you paraphrased: each part, in its own special way, helps the other parts, so that the whole body is healthy and growing, full of love.

Paul speaks here of the joints. What makes your arm operate like it does? There is a joint in the middle. How come your fingers go like that? Because there are joints. The Greek word for "joint" is *harmos*. That is the word from which we get our word "harmony."

Paul is saying that the body is to be flexible, and the body is to work together—to be coordinated. I was watching football, and I saw a man go down the field and leap 10,000 miles high and catch a ball with soft fingertips. To me, that was a work of art! I saw that man's entire body cooperating to catch a bag full of air that really does not make much difference.

We are in business for Jesus, and don't you forget it. If my ministry makes difficulty for your ministry, there is something wrong with what you, or I, or both of us are doing. My desire and prayer for our churches is that we will be one in the bond of love.

And God's people said, "Amen."

A STEADFAST CHURCH

It is obvious Satan does not want your church to succeed, to be mightily used by God. Satan has all kinds of machinations and devices and tricks to stop, slow down, or discourage the people of God.

You might think, "I don't feel any satanic opposition." Don't brag about it. If you and the devil have never met head-on, it is because you and the devil are going in the same direction. Turn around, and rather than being in collusion with him, you will be in collision with him.

Opposition from Satan is always there—and that does not mean that God is not for us. Paul said, "For a great and effective door has opened to me, and there are many adversaries" (1 Corinthians 16:9). The door to the room of opportunity swings on the hinges of opposition. There is no cheap way, no easy way, no lazy way. When you try to do something for God, and endeavor to let God use you, you *are* going to meet satanic opposition.

A CHARACTER SKETCH OF SATAN

Think of the words the Bible uses to describe the devil. He is described as a *deceiver*, a *liar*, a *murderer*, an *accuser*, a *tempter*, a *destroyer*. He has many aliases, but Satan has one desire: to dishonor and discredit the Church of the Lord Jesus Christ and every member of it.

Ephesians 6:11 speaks of "the wiles of the devil." That word "wiles" comes from the Greek *methodeias*, from which we also get the word "method." Second Corinthians 2:11 speaks of his "devices." Again in 2 Timothy 2:26 we hear about "the snare of the devil."

Wiles. Devices. Snares. Lies. Temptation. Destroyer. Evil one. Put them all together, and that will give you some idea of who is against us.

Therefore, it is all the more important that we remember Who is for us.

NEHEMIAH AND THE CHURCH

In this look at the devices of the devil—and overcoming his devices—I will take the Book of Nehemiah as our basis. Take what applied to Nehemiah so long ago and apply it to your church today.

Nehemiah was a man of God.

The Jews had been carried away into captivity, and Nehemiah got a message about the terrible condition of Jerusalem. Jerusalem is a city with beautiful walls, but those walls had fallen, and Nehemiah was heartbroken because the walls symbolized protection, separation, and beauty—the things God has for His people.

Nehemiah wanted to rebuild the walls. "So they said, 'Let us rise up and build'" (Nehemiah 2:18b).

But there were some local enemies who did not want it to happen. So, when God's man said, "Let us rise up and build," they said, "Let us rise up and stop them." There is *always* satanic opposition.

Satan is going to use his wiles and snares and devices

against your church—and to be forewarned is to be forearmed. Here are some ways the devil will try to stop the Church.

EXPECT DERISION

But it so happened, when Sanballat heard that we were rebuilding the wall, that he was furious and very indignant, and mocked the Jews. (Nehemiah 4:1).

Your church will be in derision if you stand for Christ. Do you know what a Christian is in today's society? He is called a "do-gooder," a "blue-nosed Puritan," a "fundamentalist," a "fanatic." Because of those of us who have taken a stand for righteousness, the heartland of America has been nicknamed "Jesus Land." I think it is a pretty good title, myself, but it is meant as a term of derision by those who are mocking Americans who believe in the Lord Jesus Christ.

There is no way you can stand for Jesus without becoming the laughingstock of this world. Do you think you are better than Jesus? "And they ridiculed Him" (Mark 5:40a). When Jesus was being crucified, "The men who held Jesus mocked Him and beat Him" (Luke 22:63). Not only did they mercilessly beat Him; they were laughing while they did it. "The soldiers also mocked Him, coming and offering Him sour wine, and saying, 'If You are the King of the Jews, save Yourself'" (Luke 23:36-37).

You are not better than Jesus. If they mocked the Lord Jesus, they will mock you.

Ridicule has sting. Not one of us wants to be laughed at. A Christian husband or wife who tries to live for Jesus may be mocked by his or her spouse. Students, if you go away to school and stand up for the Lord Jesus Christ and let the banners unfold and stand on the Word of God, I can promise you that you will be laughed at. If you are a businessman and you try to stand for the principles of the Lord and Savior Jesus Christ, this world is going to mock you.

FIRST OF ALL, SANBALLAT RIDICULED THE FEEBLENESS OF GOD'S PEOPLE

> *And he spoke before his brethren and the army of Samaria, and said, "What are these feeble Jews doing?"* **(Nehemiah 4:2a).**

In other words, "Look: they are insignificant, and weak." From the world's viewpoint, the Church does not have any strength. The world boasts of its power, its education, its erudition, its influence. People look at us Christians and just sort of tolerate us.

I once heard about a man who applied for a job as a lumberman. This man was about 120 pounds, and 5'6".

They said, "Look, being a lumberjack is a hard job. You've got to have great strength."

He said, "I can cut down trees."

They said, "Oh, can you? There's a sapling; cut it down!"

He took his axe, and the sapling fell.

They said, "Well, that's all right, but try this on a larger tree."

That one fell.

"Try it on this great big tree."

That one fell.

They said, "Good night! Where did you learn to chop down trees?"

The man said, "The Sahara Forest."

They said, "You mean the Sahara Desert?"

"Yeah...now!"

It is easy to underestimate the Church of the Lord Jesus Christ. Jesus started out with twelve unlettered fishermen, and went out against the imperial might of Rome, and the religious bigotry of His day, and turned that world upside down.

SECONDLY, SANBALLAT MOCKED THE FUTILITY OF THE TASK

> *Will they fortify themselves? Will they offer sacrifices? Will they complete it in a day? Will they revive the stones from the heaps of rubbish—stones that are burned? (Nehemiah 4:2b).*

The Jews were looked upon as impractical dreamers, visionaries, wasting their time with an impossible task. Therefore, their enemies laughed at them.

They also laughed at the foolishness of their faith.

Look in the verse above: "*Will they sacrifice?*" Sanballat is saying, "Are they going to worship their God?" Their devotion to the God of Heaven was a source of ridicule.

What we believe—the old-fashioned, old-time religion; the truth of God's Word, and its inerrancy and impeccability; the deity of Jesus, and His blood sacrifice; the things that we hold dear—people laugh at. It has always been that way. "For the message of the cross is foolishness to those who are perishing" (1 Corinthians 1:18a).

Harry Ironsides used to be the pastor of Moody Memorial Church in Chicago. Once he and some friends were out in Oakland, California, on a ferry crossing. They were singing choruses and praising the Lord.

A man standing there said, "Who are you?"

Harry Ironsides said, "We are some Christians."

"What are you doing?"

"We're praising the Lord."

The man said, "You're fools."

Ironsides said, "Yes, that's true. We are fools." But he said, "We are fools for Christ's sake. Whose fool are you?"

Why do they ridicule us? The reason a person laughs at holy things is because he is a wicked person. "Scoffers will come in the last days, walking according to their own lusts" (2 Peter 3:3b). Show me a scoffer—like Sanballat and Tobiah in Nehemiah 4—who laughs at God's Word and God's people, and I will show you someone who has the devil's initials carved in his heart, someone who is covered with the slimy fingerprints of sin. The reason people scoff is because of the character they have.

Consider the company you are in when they laugh at you. You are no better than Jesus. If they mocked the Lord Jesus, they are going to mock you. Now, if nobody is laughing at you, if you have *not* been ridiculed, perhaps Satan does not think you are worthy of worry. But if you are getting some flack, it just may be that you are over the target.

Consider the reward that is yours for being laughed at! Jesus said,

> *Blessed are you when they revile and persecute you, and say all kinds of evil against you falsely for My sake. Rejoice and be exceedingly glad, for great is your reward in heaven, for so they persecuted the prophets who were before you (Matthew 5:11-12).*

If somebody laughs at you because of your faith, you ought to go home and throw a party. Say, "How wonderful it is that people can see a difference in me!"

EXPECT DISCOURAGEMENT

Then Judah [one of the Jewish leaders] said, "The strength of the laborers is failing, and there is so much rubbish that we are not able to build the wall" (Nehemiah 4:10, words in brackets added).

They were discouraged, and the discouragement did not come from the outside. This time, Satan used somebody from the inside.

Discouragement is one of life's most deadly diseases. It is universal, and it is recurring, but thank God, it *can* be cured.

What are the causes of discouragement?

WORN OUT

They were worn out. "The strength of the laborers is failing…"

Sometimes we get tired. Vince Lombardi, the famous former coach of the Green Bay Packers, said, "Fatigue makes cowards of us all." Sometimes the most spiritual thing we can do is go to bed. Did you know that?

When did this discouragement come to the Jews? When they were half done, right in the middle of the work. "So we built the wall, and the entire wall was joined together up to half its height…" (Nehemiah 4:6a).

Do you ever start to climb a mountain—or even a mole hill—and get about halfway up, and decide it's not a good idea? You have heard of "midlife crisis," when you come to a certain stage in your life when you say, "I'm not going to be able to do the things that I thought I ought to do. I'm not going to be able to make it." Did you ever buy a new car? The newness wears off about the time the car is half paid for. This always happens to us.

WEIGHED DOWN

Not only were they worn out; they were weighed down. "... there is so much rubbish that we are not able to build the wall" (Nehemiah 4:10b).

Your church will face rubbish. You, personally, will face rubbish. Serving the Lord Jesus Christ is not always glamorous. You cannot build without stones, but those stones are sometimes buried in rubbish. But you cannot build on rubbish, either.

Church, listen: it is not going to be all easy, all honey and no bees. If the devil cannot laugh you out of service to the Lord Jesus Christ, then he will try to discourage you. He will come when the job is half done and say, "You are worn out. You are weighed down. It cannot be done!"

It is sad when this comes from within. Some people are like a drink of water to a drowning man. I have had people discourage me—or try to, anyway.

I pastored a little church on the Gulf Coast of Mississippi when I was in seminary. We met in a little army barracks building. We had about 50 members, and 25 of them were crooks. I'm serious! It was not much. We got the crooks straightened out after a while, but it was a hard little church to pastor. I knew that we needed to grow, that we needed more buildings. But we did not have any money, and hardly any leadership in that church.

But I went to Nashville, to our Sunday School Board, and got some architectural plans that I thought would fit that church. I got three shovels. I got two other young men, and I said, "Let's mark off the foundation of this building, and begin to dig." We had no money! No builders! No help! We got out there in the blazing sun and began to dig the footing of that building.

One of the leading members of that church came by. She said, "What are you doing?"

We said, "We are digging the footing for our new building."

She said, "It will never be done."

I said to myself, "Oh yes, it will!"

Friend, that building got built.

There are those who tell you that it cannot be done, but it *can* be done. Do not let the devil talk you out of a work for the Lord Jesus Christ!

EXPECT DISMAY

And our adversaries said, "They will neither know nor see anything, till we come into their midst and kill them and cause the work to cease" (Nehemiah 4:11).

Terrorism is not new. If Satan cannot laugh or discourage you away from work for God, he will try to threaten you away.

Satan is not always dainty. He is not above taking your life or inciting somebody to kill you. In my ministry, I have had not a few death threats. I have been the target of wicked people.

Friend, if they sought to put our Lord to death, do you not think they will want to put us to death? Jesus said, "Yes, the time is coming that whoever kills you will think that he offers God service" (John 16:2b). Satan will stop at nothing.

What do you do when Satan comes to dismay you, to frighten you from a work for God? Do what Nehemiah did.

REMEMBER THE LORD

> *And I looked, and arose and said to the nobles, to the leaders, and to the rest of the people, "Do not be afraid of them. Remember the Lord, great and awesome..."* **(Nehemiah 4:14a).**

I got a call one day from the Sheriff's Department. They said, "Pastor, there is a man with a rifle who said he is coming down there to kill you. We don't know where he is, but we just need to tell you."

I was sitting in my study. I said, "Lord, what do You want me to do?" I thought, *first, I'm going to get a word from the Word.* I keep my Bible open to Psalm 119 in my study, because that psalm is about the Bible, and about preaching. Before I step out, many times I will just glance at it.

So, I walked over there, and I put my finger down. But it was not on Psalm 119; it was Psalm 118. I had put my finger down on the wrong page—but it was the right page. I looked down and saw: "I shall not die, but live, and declare the works of the Lord" (Psalm 118:17).

I said, "Well, that's a good verse."

People say, "Haven't people been killed for serving Jesus?" Of course they have. Does that mean they lost? No, that means they won! "And they overcame him by the blood of the Lamb and by the word of their testimony, and they did not love their lives to the death" (Revelation 12:11).

The time is going to come when to be a Bible-believing Christian will be dangerous. So, as Nehemiah said to his people, "Remember the Lord."

REMEMBER WHAT'S AT STAKE

Do not be afraid of them. Remember the Lord, great and awesome, and fight for your brethren, your sons, your daughters, your wives, and your houses (Nehemiah 4:14b).

Reflect on the issues at stake. Remember your sons, your daughters, your wives, your houses! *Stand up for Jesus, ye soldiers of the cross.* Resist the enemy.

Every one of the builders had his sword girded at his side as he built (Nehemiah 4:18a).

They were building and battling at the same time...and so must you be! The devil would like to terrify you, but the Bible says be "not in any way terrified by your adversaries" (Philippians 1:28a).

To the contrary, "Resist the devil and he will flee from you" (James 4:7b). It is not enough for you to say, "I am not afraid of the devil." The devil ought to be afraid of *you*—a man armed in the power and the anointing of Almighty God.

EXPECT DISCORD

And there was a great outcry of the people and their wives against their Jewish brethren (Nehemiah 5:1).

Here, these Jews are supposed to be building, and they turn against one another. If Satan cannot intimidate us with bodily harm or humiliate us with laughter, he will try to sow discord among the brethren. That is why we preach that we must have a unified Church. The devil would rather start a church fuss than open a porno palace. Are you going to let Satan divide you as a church? No!

So, there was discord among the Jews. Do you know what it was over? Finances. Some people did not like the way the finances were being handled—and frankly, they were not doing the best job.

But you have to watch people who get upset over finances in a church. There is a time, obviously, when people need to be held to account. But there is another category of people who nitpick. Every church has its own kind of self-styled watchdog.

One man in a particular church opened the broom closet one day, and there were five brand new brooms. He got upset and asked the janitor, "Whoever authorized anybody to buy five brooms at one time? We're not meeting our budget, and here are five brand new brooms!"

The janitor said, "I don't know. Maybe you ought to ask the pastor."

The man, very irate, came in to talk to the pastor. "Why do we have five brand new brooms in the closet?"

The pastor said, "Maybe there was a sale on brooms? I don't know."

Later, the pastor was having coffee with the church treasurer, and mentioned this.

The treasurer just smiled and said, "Oh pastor, that's easy to understand. How would you feel if you saw everything you had given to the church in the past year tied up in five brooms?"

Church, there are no problems too big to solve—only people too small to solve them.

EXPECT DISTRACTION

> *Now it happened when Sanballat, Tobiah, Geshem the Arab, and the rest of our enemies heard that I had rebuilt the wall, and that there were no breaks left in it (though at that time I had not hung the doors in the gates), that Sanballat and Geshem sent to me, saying, "Come, let us meet together among the villages in the plain of Ono." But they thought to do me harm.*
>
> *So I sent messengers to them, saying, "I am doing a great work, so that I cannot come down. Why should the work cease while I leave it and go down to you?"* (Nehemiah 6:1-3).

They really did not want to help Nehemiah. They wanted to distract him from the work.

Satan will try to distract the Church. What is our purpose? Why are we built? Why are we here? To magnify Jesus through worship and the Word, to move believers in Jesus toward maturity and ministry, and to make Jesus known to our neighbors and the nations. The devil will try to get us to do something else, to come aside and sit down and *talk* about these things. Nehemiah said, "I can't do it. I am doing a great work, and I will not come down."

Do not ever let your church get distracted. We are here to glorify Jesus and to win souls. Amen.

Some of you mothers are doing a great work as a mother to your children. But somebody says, "You need to stop that, and go out and get a job." If you have to do that to put food on the table or clothes on the back, you have to do it. But if you are a mother raising little children, you *are* doing a great work! The devil will say, "Step down."

Some of you who used to serve the Lord Jesus Christ in church are not serving now—but you are members of other clubs and organizations. Why is that? Why have you allowed the devil to distract you? Get out of some of those things that do not really matter. Stay with the Church. You are doing a great work. Do not come down!

EXPECT DEFAMATION

Then Sanballat sent his servant to me as before, the fifth time, with an open letter in his hand. In it was written:
"It is reported among the nations, and Geshem says, that you and the Jews plan to rebel; therefore, according to these rumors, you are rebuilding the wall, that you may be their king. And you have also appointed prophets to proclaim concerning you at Jerusalem, saying, 'There is a king in Judah!' Now these matters will be reported to the king. So come, therefore, and let us consult together."
Then I sent to him, saying, "No such things as you say are being done, but you invent them in your own heart" (Nehemiah 6:5-8).

Here was a vicious rumor to defame Nehemiah. They said, "We know why you're building these walls: you are building a kingdom for yourself."

Have you ever heard anybody say, "That pastor is motivated by personal ambition"? That's what they said about Nehemiah. "He doesn't really love God. He is not really doing a spiritual thing. He is trying to set himself up as king."

Notice how they spread this rumor: "And Geshem says..." Some individual said it. This was an open letter, very much like a letter to the editor, to defame God's people. You are never more like the devil than when you spread rumors about godly people.

A little 3-year-old had heard the Lord's Prayer. She did not quite get it right: "And forgive us our trash baskets, as we forgive others who put trash in our baskets." Don't let somebody put trash in your basket! These are people who say things they have no business saying.

One godly pastor was doing a good job, but two men in the church did not like him. They came to him and said, "Pastor, we think you should no longer be the pastor in this church. We're asking you to resign."

He said, "Gentlemen, thank you for coming to me. I'll tell you what I'll do: I will take it to the Lord and pray over it, and I'll get back with you."

Next week came, and they met, and the men said, "Well, what did God say to you?"

The pastor said, "God said He had never heard of you two."

There are always people who will be used by the devil to defame the good.

Satan will do everything he can do to get you to come down from the wall. And by God's grace, you are not going to do it! You are going to be God's people, and you are not going to let derision, discouragement, division, dismay, or defamation, or any other thing keep you from being a steadfast church.

A SPIRIT-FILLED CHURCH

I heard about a man who was working in his woodworking shop and nicked his finger.

His wife said, "You better go down to the medical place and have them take a look at that."

So, he drove down there and went in the front door. Not a soul was in the room. He saw two other doors: one said *Male*, and the other said *Female*. He said, "I'm a male," so he went in that door.

Then he saw two more doors: *Over 60*, and *Under 60*. He said, "I'm over 60," and went in that door.

Two more doors: *Minor*, and *Major*. He said, "Well, this is minor," so he went in that door.

More doors: *Above the Waist*, or *Below the Waist*. He said, "Well...I think it's above the waist if I hold it up this way..." He went through that door–and he was back out in the alley.

He came home. His wife said, "Did they help you?"

He said, "No, but they sure were organized!"

People come to church that way. We process them, we grade them, we put them here and there. They come in one door, and they go out the other door, but there is no radical, dramatic change. When you worship God, you ought to be changed.

Jesus said that we are to be in a wonderful business.

> **"Most assuredly, I say to you, he who believes in Me, the works that I do he will do also; and greater works than these he will do, because I go to My Father" (John 14:12).**

"He who believes in Me." There are only two classes of people: believers and unbelievers. Do you say that you believe? Are you doing the works of Jesus—and greater works? If not, something is wrong, and it is not Scripture.

I heard about a battle where the flag-bearer got out in front of the regiment in enemy territory. Someone said to the captain, "Shall we bring the flag back to the regiment?" The captain said, "No. Bring the regiment up to the flag."

When we read a Scripture like John 14:12, we are tempted to bring the flag back to where we are, to dumb it down so that it fits our experience. But Jesus said that if anyone believes in Him, "greater works than these he will do."

Here are four things to lay to heart regarding what it means to be a Spirit-filled Church.

OUR PROGRAM

What is the Church's program? It is not an activities program, nor a music program, nor an educational program. The Church's program is to do the works of Jesus, and to excel the works of Jesus.

How can we do the works of Jesus...much less excel them? Jesus walked on water! Jesus raised the dead!

What our Lord is talking about in John 14:12 is not raising the dead. When He is talking about "greater works," He is not talking about quality; He is talking about *quantity*. He is talking about leading people to Himself. He is talking about evangelism, soul-winning, multiplication. Bringing a soul to Jesus Christ is greater than raising a man from the dead.

Turn backward to John 5. Again, Jesus is talking about greater works.

> *"For the Father loves the Son, and shows Him all things that He Himself does; and He will show Him greater works than these, that you may marvel....Most assuredly, I say to you, he who hears My word and believes in Him who sent Me has everlasting life, and shall not come into judgment, but has passed from death into life" (John 5:20, 24).*

Even the people that Jesus raised, died again. But when we believe in Him, when we trust Him, we have everlasting life. Do you want to see a miracle? Look at a believer in Jesus. You are looking at a man who cannot die.

Which is the greater work: to raise a man from the dead, or to help a man come to the Lord Jesus Christ, so that he can never die? These "greater works" refer to the salvation ministry of Christ.

"Jesus said to them, 'My food is to do the will of Him who sent Me, and to finish His work'" (John 4:34). What did God send Jesus to do? To heal the sick? To feed the hungry? "The Son of Man has come to seek and to save that which was lost" (Luke 19:10). Jesus came not as the great healer, nor as the great teacher. He is those things, but He *came* as Savior.

> *Jesus spoke these words, lifted up His eyes to heaven, and said: "Father, the hour has come. Glorify Your Son, that Your Son also may glorify You, as You have given*

***Him authority over all flesh, that He should give eternal life to as many as You have given Him. And this is eternal life, that they may know You, the only true God, and Jesus Christ whom You have sent. I have glorified You on the earth. I have finished the work which You have given Me to do"* (John 17:1-4).**

Do you see it? The work of God is to bring souls to Jesus Christ, and that glorifies God.

Remember, when Jesus said, "he who believes in Me... greater works than these he will do"? (See John 14:12, above.) Again, He is not talking about "greater" in quality, but in quantity. We, as a Church, are going to do far more than Jesus did when He was on this Earth walking in the flesh.

At Pentecost, more souls were saved in one day than came to Jesus in His entire ministry. "Then those who gladly received his word were baptized; and that day about three thousand souls were added to them" (Acts 2:41). What our Lord wants is multiplied souls coming to Him.

Church, God wants you to be a part of it. God wants your church to be Spirit-filled, doing the works of Jesus—that is, giving eternal life.

Do you believe in Jesus? This is your program. Preaching, choirs, educational programs are fine, but they all are only a part of a great program, and that is doing the works of Jesus. Never minimize bringing souls to Jesus Christ. There is no substitute. If a church moves away from evangelism, it signs its death warrant. Your church exists by evangelism like a fire exists by burning.

OUR PROMISE

In John 14, verses 12 and 13 are conjoined.

> *"...And greater works than these he will do, because I go to My Father. And whatever you ask in My name, that I will do, that the Father may be glorified in the Son"* **(John 14:12b-13).**

How do we do these greater works? Through believing prayer. On the Day of Pentecost, they had prayed for 10 days, preached for 15 minutes, and 3,000 got saved. We pray for 10 minutes and preach for 10 days, and have a handful saved. Our exciting program of evangelism is based upon a promise: that God will answer our prayer.

Prayer is not a substitute for our work. Prayer is not preliminary to our work. In many senses, prayer *is* our work. Do you believe that God will do greater things through your prayer? This next question will be embarrassing: How much, then, do you pray? You can do a lot without prayer. The pyramids were built without prayer to our true God. But the greater works that Jesus commands His Church to do must be done by prayer.

Notice what kind of prayer it is:

THE RIGHT PEOPLE

John 14:12 tells us it must be "he who believes in Me." If you are not a believer, your prayer does not get any higher than the lightbulbs. But if you believe, if you know the Lord Jesus Christ, you are the right person.

If you do not find in your heart an earnest desire to pray, I wonder if you *are* saved—because, "God has sent forth the Spirit of His Son into your hearts, crying out, 'Abba, Father!'" (Galatians 4:6b).

THE RIGHT POWER

"And whatever you ask in My name, that I will do" (John 14:13a). You cannot just forge Jesus' name to a prayer. "In the name of Jesus, I want a swimming pool." What does it mean to ask in His name?

The name stands for authority. You put your name on a check. That gives the cashier the authority to take some money out of the bank and hand it to you, because you have some in your account. If you do not have anything in your account, and you put your name on that check, they don't put the check in jail—they put *you* in jail, because your name stands for you.

If you ask anything in Jesus' name—that is, with His authority and His approval—then He will do it.

Maybe there is a wild party, and a policeman goes and knocks on the door. "Open up, in the name of the law." He might weigh 150 pounds, but he has a badge on. He has authority. We, as believers, do not have to have physical strength, monetary strength, or intellectual superiority. We have the authority of Jesus Christ.

THE RIGHT PURPOSE

Now suppose that policeman goes home and says to his neighbor, "May I borrow your lawnmower, in the name of the law?" That doesn't fit, does it? He cannot take that authority and apply it where it does not belong.

"In the name of Jesus" means for the right purpose. What is the right purpose? "Whatever you ask in My name, that I will do, that the Father may be glorified in the Son" (John 14:13). The purpose of prayer is to glorify God. It is not to have our little selfish desires met.

When you get the right person praying with the right power, here is how to get your prayers answered: let your purpose and God's purpose come together—for God to be glorified.

We are to do greater works than the Lord Jesus Christ, and the way we do that is through believing prayer. God has given us an explicit promise. Do not take from it. Do not add to it. Believe it and practice it.

OUR PRACTICE

"If you love Me, keep My commandments" (John 14:15).

If you say that you love the Lord Jesus Christ and you are not keeping His commandments, you are a liar. If you do not keep His commandments, it is no wonder you are not doing greater works.

What is His commandment? The Great Commission.

"Go therefore and make disciples of all the nations, baptizing them in the name of the Father and of the Son and of the Holy Spirit..." (Matthew 28:19).

What are the greater works? Bringing people to Jesus Christ. Jesus said, "You shall receive power when the Holy Spirit has come upon you; and you shall be witnesses to Me" (Acts 1:8a).

He did not say that you are to go out and argue. You might say, "I don't know a lot of theology. I cannot witness."

Yes, you can! If you are saved, if you believe in Jesus, you can witness. You know how you got saved, don't you? Can't you tell somebody else how you got saved?

Our Lord has not called you to be a lawyer, but a witness. A lawyer argues a case; a witness tells what he has seen and heard. The only reason some people do not witness is that they have not seen or heard anything. With the first soul that I ever led to Christ, all I did was tell him how I got saved—and he got saved. It was very simple, glorious, and wonderful.

There is no cheap, easy, lazy way to do it. A bullet does not make a martyr; it just reveals one. You say, "Oh, I would die for Jesus!" Put that on the shelf. Will you *live* for Jesus? The word "witness" and the word "martyr" are the same word in the Greek language.

Jesus said, "If you love me, keep my commandments" (John 14:15). That is the Church's expected practice. Over and over in the Bible, Jesus tells us that we are to share Him.

Whatever manpower and ability your church may have, there is still a sense of failure if there is not a soul-winning heart in the life of your people. A lot of people think they have done God a wild favor when they get to church on Sunday morning. You ask them, "Do you serve Jesus?" They answer, "I go to church."

You are to do the works of Jesus, and greater works. You are expected to obey the Lord if you love Him.

OUR POWER

> *"And I will pray the Father, and He will give you another Helper, that He may abide with you forever—the Spirit of truth, whom the world cannot receive, because it neither*

sees Him nor knows Him; but you know Him, for He dwells with you and will be in you" (John 14:16-17).

Who was dwelling with them? Jesus. Who would be in them? Jesus. "I will not leave you orphans; I will come to you" (John 14:18). The Holy Spirit is Christ in the Christian.

We have a mission impossible: we are to do the works that Jesus did, and greater works. So, Jesus said, "Pray, and obey, and I am going to send you another Helper, another Comforter."

The word "Helper" is the word "paraclete" (Greek *parakletos*), which means somebody who will come alongside you, someone who will get into the yoke with you, to empower and strengthen you. You will never be alone.

Jesus uses the word "another." There are two Greek words for "another." For example, one of them might mean, "I've got a horse, but I need another horse." The other means another of a different kind—as in, "I've got a horse, but I'm going to get a car."

Here, Jesus uses the Greek word that means *another of the same kind*. He says, "I will send you another Helper, the Holy Spirit." And then He says, "I will come to you." Do you get it?

In a Christian, Jesus lives again. That is the way we can do the works that Jesus did, and the greater works. Jesus said, "Whatever you ask in My name, that I will do" (John 14:13a). He did not say He would help you to do it. He said, "I will do it."

God moves in and begins to work in you, through you, and with you. When you believe Him for greater works than raising the dead, when you pray believing prayer in the name and authority of Jesus for the glory of God, when you obey Him when He says, "Be witnesses to me," then God will empower you. God sends another comforter, the Holy Spirit, who is Jesus Christ in you.

Stuart Briscoe, a preacher friend of mine, said, "When I first got saved, I was so full of joy. I walked out and said, 'Man, this is easy!'" Then after he lived a while and got his nose bumped a few times, he said, "This is difficult." As he repented and tried to get better and stronger, and made more resolutions and failed more, he said, "This is impossible." But then he learned the secret of Christ in him—and he said, "This is wonderful."

There is only one who has ever lived the Christian life. His name is Jesus. If the Christian life is lived in your house, in your club, on your team, in your choir, there is only one person who will be doing it. Jesus!

We are not to be little tin imitations of Jesus. It is Christ *in us*. Oh God, help us to understand this, that Jesus Christ is alive in me! He is the one who steps in. *This* is the exceeding power that we have, to do these greater works than the Lord Jesus Christ.

How many of us would say, "I just wish I could have been here when Jesus was on Earth. I wish I could have walked with Jesus, breathed that air, and been there during the miracle times."

> **"Nevertheless I tell you the truth. It is to your advantage that I go away; for if I do not go away, the Helper will not come to you; but if I depart, I will send Him to you" (John 16:7).**

When Jesus left this Earth and went back to Heaven, that was glorious because He then sent the Spirit to take His place. What is the difference?

When Jesus was here on Earth, He was limited by time and space. "Martha said to Jesus, 'Lord, if You had been here, my brother would not have died'" (John 11:21). If He were here, He could not be there. But when He comes with the Holy Spirit, Jesus is with me, with them, and with you, and He is not limited by space. He is not limited by time. He lives and dwells in all of us through the Holy Spirit of God, and therefore, the Church is the visible body of the invisible Christ, and Christ is the invisible person of the visible Church.

How can we do the works of Jesus, and greater works? Because He will still be doing the works, but He will now do them in you, and me, and our brothers and sisters in Christ. Do not cop out. This is the work of the whole Church, for the whole age.

There are three miracles in the Christian's life. The first miracle is the new birth, when you get saved. The third miracle will be when you are glorified at the Rapture, the resurrection, when you are made like the Lord Jesus. But there is a middle miracle, and that is when you and I live day by day empowered by the Holy Spirit, and can say with the Apostle Paul, "I have been crucified with Christ; it is no longer I who live, but Christ lives in me" (Galatians 2:20a).

My heartbeat prayer for the Church is that we will be obedient to the Lord Jesus Christ, and God will look down from Heaven with a smile and say, "They are doing greater works, because they believe in Me, because they pray and obey, and I dwell in them."

Do you think you understand this? If so, that is good. But it would be far better for you *not* to understand it, than to understand it and not obey it.

Present yourself to the Lord right now, and say, "Lord God, here I am. I am available. I will obey. Empower me with Your blessed, precious Holy Spirit to do the job."

A FINAL CHARGE TO THE CHURCH

A PRAYING CHURCH

Your church will be no greater, no better, no more useful than her prayer life. And her prayer life is not going to be any better than *your* prayer life, because you are the Church.

Do not ask, "Is my church a praying church?"

Ask yourself, "Am I a praying Christian?"

If you could ask the Lord Jesus Christ for anything you wanted, what would you ask? Would you say, "Lord, teach me to preach," or, "Teach me to sing," or, "Teach me to lead"?

The disciples asked this: "Lord, teach us to pray." Listen to the Lord's answer.

> *"Ask, and it will be given to you; seek, and you will find; knock, and it will be opened to you. For everyone who asks receives, and he who seeks finds, and to him who knocks it will be opened" (Matthew 7:7-8).*

These are the words of Jesus: an undeniable, impeccable promise. Our Lord says we are to ask, seek, and knock.

When we ask, that speaks of our desires. When we seek, that speaks of God's direction. And when we knock, that speaks of determination. We need to bring desire, direction, and determination together into a burning laser point to get our prayers answered before God.

The greatest problem you have in your life is not unanswered prayer; it is unoffered prayer. "You do not have because you do not ask" (James 4:2c). Not to pray is not only to miss a blessing; it is rebellious. Our Lord has commanded us to pray.

"Men always ought to pray and not lose heart" (Luke 18:1b). Who said that? Jesus. He also said, "Watch and pray, lest you enter into temptation" (Mark 14:38a).

The Apostle Paul said, "Be anxious for nothing, but in everything by prayer and supplication, with thanksgiving, let your requests be made known to God" (Philippians 4:6).

There is no substitute for intercession and prayer—not enthusiasm, not eloquence, not energy. The reason many of us fail, the reason many of us are poverty-stricken in our spiritual lives, is that we have never learned to pray. May God help you to pray, so that your church will be a praying church!

WHY DOES GOD ASK US TO PRAY?

It's a good question. Isn't God good? Doesn't God want to do good things? And doesn't God know everything? "For your Father knows the things you have need of before you ask Him" (Matthew 6:8b). That just begs the question, then: why should we ask?

We do not pray to impress God. Do not use vain repetition. Jesus said, "And when you pray, do not use vain repetitions as the heathen do. For they think that they will be heard for their many words" (Matthew 6:7). You do not have to be a junior-size Shakespeare with flowery praises.

We do not pray to inform God. God already knows what things we need. There is nothing that you can tell Him that He does not already know.

We do not pray to instruct God. Prayer is not some way of bending God's will to fit yours.

We *pray to invite God*—so that we can delight ourselves in the Lord. Second Corinthians 6:1 says that we are "workers together with Him." God loves us so much that He gives us the privilege of participating in His kingdom work, through prayer.

God can work without our prayers, but we cannot work without God. It is prayer that causes us to depend upon Him.

If He simply blessed us without our asking, what would that do? That would teach us to live life independently from God. But Jesus said, "If you abide in Me, and My words abide in you, you will ask what you desire, and it shall be done for you" (John 15:7). That is the reason God has taught us to pray: to invite Him to take control of our lives.

The devil cannot keep God from answering. So, he will endeavor to keep you from asking.

ASK: EXPRESS YOUR DESIRES TO GOD
If you have a desire in your heart:

> *"Therefore I say to you, whatever things you ask when you pray, believe that you receive them, and you will have them" (Mark 11:24).*

Do not get the idea that there are spiritual things that you can ask for, and secular things that you cannot ask for. The Bible never divides life between the sacred and the secular. With God, every task is a holy task, every day is a holy day. Can you imagine Jesus saying, "Father, when I preach, I want anointing, but the rest of the time I will do it Myself"? No. "In *everything* by prayer and supplication, with thanksgiving, let your requests be made known to God" (Philippians 4:6b, emphasis added).

> "*Delight yourself also in the* LORD, *and He shall give you the desires of your heart*" (Psalm 37:4).

A good test as to whether you should desire it or whether you should do it is, can you ask God to do it through you? Whatever you desire, tell God. Ask.

"What if I want the wrong thing?" Tell Him. Say, "Lord, I want the wrong thing. Have mercy upon me, oh God! Fix my want-er." You cannot hide it from God. If you want it, He already knows it, doesn't He? So, tell Him.

Pray about everything. The responsibility for asking is ours. The responsibility for giving is God's.

Learn these three words today: *direct*, *different*, and *delayed*.

I once went to a presidential inauguration, and I had a wonderful time. But at first, I did not have a ticket. So, I called our senators' office and said, "I need a ticket."

They sent a ticket, but said, "We need to tell you, it is standing, and you will be a third of a mile back." No exaggeration!

So, I asked another friend for a better ticket. He said, "Yes, you're supposed to have a better ticket, in a seated area. I have sent it over to the hotel."

I went to the hotel. It was not there. I went again. Not there. It was time for the inaugural event. I was sitting out in the lobby, and Dr. James Dobson came around the corner. He said, "What are you doing?"

"A man was supposed to send some tickets over here for me, and they haven't come."

"Well," Dr. Dobson's friend said, "look: I've got four tickets." These were for the best seats in the house. I had my daughter and son-in-law with me, in nice chairs on a cement platform.

Just before I was given those tickets, I prayed, "Lord, I don't have to have those tickets, and I am no better than anybody else in this city. There is no reason that I should have the privilege of getting a closer seat or having a chair to sit on—but I want one. God, I don't know that this is Your will. I cannot pray in the name of Jesus. This is just what I *want*. Lord, I'm Your child, and that's what I want."

I had not prayed that prayer two or three minutes before they came around the corner, and I had in my hand four of the best seats in the place. I asked God, and the answer was direct. Do not think some things are too big or too small for God to answer.

Down in Florida, one time, I got to go fishing in the saltwater lagoon called the Indian River with some pals. I love to fish, especially in salt water, and I had not been fishing for a long time.

We were wading on the sandbar, casting for speckled trout, and I was talking to the Lord all by myself, away from everybody else—just loving Him and praising Him. And I said, "Lord, I am not catching any fish. I have not been fishing for a long time, and it may be a long time before I go fishing again. Lord, I want to catch a great big trout. Not a small one, but a big one." I told Him this! I said, "I cannot ask in Jesus' name. I have no right to catch a big fish. It is not a necessity. But I want one."

Not any longer than two minutes later, I dropped that lure down into a deep hole off that sandbar and began to bring it up—and I saw a big yellow mouth coming up out of the water. That big, speckled trout hit that lure, and I wrestled him all over the waterscape out there. Finally, I got him landed, and it was a prize trout.

Immediately after I prayed for this fish, God gave the answer. I said, "Lord, that was great. I want another one." I cast for another one. In two or three more minutes, I had caught another huge trout. I stopped asking, and I stopped catching.

What was God doing? He knew the desire of my heart.

I woke up one night with an excruciating pain in my right ear. What caused it, I do not know. But I put my hand on my ear, and I said, "Oh Jesus, in Your holy name, heal me." Immediately, the pain was gone. I do not know what caused it, but I know who took it. His name is Jesus.

I was driving to a revival meeting one time, in Wauchula, Florida. I was out there going along about 65 miles an hour, happy as I could be—when my car stopped running. It did not sputter. It just stopped running. I put it in neutral and coasted as far as I could. Out there all by myself on this road, I did what everybody does: I got out and looked under the hood. Well... there was the engine; it hadn't fallen out. What was wrong with that car, I do not know, but I got in and I cranked, and I cranked, and it would not even sputter, until finally my battery was going dead.

Then I thought, *Adrian, have you asked God?*

I got out and laid my hand on the hood, and I said, "Lord, if You are the Great Physician, You are also the Great Mechanic. I ask You, in the name of Jesus," (because I was going to a revival meeting), "fix my car."

I got in and turned the key. The engine roared.

You might say, "Well, that was a coincidence." You believe what you believe; I will believe what I believe. Sometimes the answer to prayer is direct. But He cannot answer unless we ask.

SEEK: EXPECT DIRECTION FROM GOD

Sometimes we ask God for things that are not His will. Why did Jesus say, "Seek"? Because God sometimes wants to redirect our prayers to His will. Asking and seeking must be linked together.

God's ways are unknown to us. Sometimes we *are* asking for one thing, and we need to be seeking another thing, so we keep asking and seeking until God directs our prayer. Have you ever thanked God for unanswered prayer?

The property on which Bellevue Baptist Church stands in Cordova, Tennessee is an answer to prayer, but not because I sought it at first.

We were trying to build a church in downtown Memphis. Had we built downtown, we would have overbuilt the area and underbuilt for our need. We had 24 acres of property, and we were trying to buy at least three more acres.

We prayed, and I stained Heaven asking God for property so that we might build a worship center where we could reach people—because at the time, we were having three services on Sunday morning, and then another again on Sunday night.

I remember I was with my friend Roland Maddox one day. He said, "You know, Pastor, that piece of property we've been trying to buy? The man has just raised the price again."

Here is what I said—I can remember the exact words: "Well, praise God. No two-legged man whose breath is in his nostrils is going to stop what God is doing. Just praise God. I don't understand the way, but praise You, Lord. Praise You."

That man did us the best favor he could have possibly done for us by raising the price on that property.

One night in Orlando, as I was trying to sleep, God laid on my heart that we need to move the entire facility out to Cordova. It has been an incredible blessing. We asked God for one thing, and we kept seeking God until He showed us what His real plan for us was.

I remember I used to pray, "God, let Interstate 40 go through Overton Park, so that our people, who live where they live, can get to the church without having to go around through Robin Hood's barn!" I explained the whole deal to the Lord. I tried to inform Him, and then instruct Him, but I did not impress Him. But He heard my prayer.

When I went and told the mayor of the city what we were about to build in Cordova, he said, "That's wonderful. You know, the money that was set aside to go through Overton Park can be used to put an interchange right there."

Isn't God good? Sometimes the answers are direct. But sometimes the answers are different.

The Apostle Paul had a spiritual thorn in the flesh.

> **...A thorn in the flesh was given to me, a messenger of Satan to buffet me, lest I be exalted above measure. Concerning this thing I pleaded with the Lord three times that it might depart from me. And He said to me, "My grace is sufficient for you, for My strength is made perfect in weakness" (2 Corinthians 12:7b-9a).**

God said, "No. I have something different for you, something better. I am going to give you a special anointing."

So, what do we do? We ask and express our desires to God. Then we seek, and experience direction from God. Third, we knock.

KNOCK: EXERCISE DETERMINATION WITH GOD

Sometimes we *are* asking in the will of God. We are asking with specificity for what God wants to give us—but we give up too easily.

To knock implies determination.

In the original Greek language, the word for "knock" in Matthew 7:7 means, "knock and keep on knocking."

Sometimes God's answers are delayed. There seems to be some impediment. We have asked God. We have sought God, but the door is closed. God says, "Keep on knocking on Heaven's door." Why would God tell us to do that? Why does God not just give us what we ask?

In Luke 11, Jesus is again teaching on prayer.

> *And He said to them, "Which of you shall have a friend, and go to him at midnight and say to him, 'Friend, lend me three loaves; for a friend of mine has come to me on his journey, and I have nothing to set before him'..." (Luke 11:5-6).*

In the Middle East, if a friend comes to you, you must invite him to stay and you must feed him. That is the expected thing. This man is saying, "My cupboard is empty. I've got to feed my friend something."

> *"...And he will answer from within and say, 'Do not trouble me; the door is now shut, and my children are with me in bed; I cannot rise and give to you'? I say to you, though he will not rise and give to him because he is his friend, yet because of his persistence he will rise and give him as many as he needs. So I say to you, ask, and it will be given to you; seek, and you will find; knock, and it will be opened to you" (Luke 11:7-9).*

Jesus is not talking here about a light rattle on the doorknob. He is talking about a man banging on the door.

His neighbor says, "Will you go away? Do you know what time it is? If you wake up those dogs and those babies, we are going to have some serious trouble." In those days, houses were small. The locks were complicated, and often the whole family slept in one room. So, the neighbor said, "Look, I can't. Go away."

Knock, knock.

"I said, go away."

Knock, knock.

"I said, how many do you need?"

Why would Jesus use an illustration like that about prayer? He is not saying that God is like an unconcerned neighbor. He is saying that if a neighbor will do what is asked just because he is being pestered, how much more will God hear us if we continue to seek, continue to ask, continue to knock!

Jesus told another story, of an unjust judge. There was a widow, who had a good case. But this crooked judge would not answer her. He did not have time for her.

She just kept on pestering him.

> **And he would not for a while; but afterward he said within himself, "Though I do not fear God nor regard man, yet because this widow troubles me I will avenge her, lest by her continual coming she weary me" (Luke 18:4-5).**

What a hard-hearted guy this was!

> **Then the Lord said, "Hear what the unjust judge said. And shall God not avenge His own elect who cry out day and night to Him, though He bears long with them? I tell you that He will avenge them speedily" (Luke 18:6-8a).**

Jesus is saying, "If even an unconcerned neighbor and an unconcerned judge will hear persistent prayer, then keep on knocking."

Over in Matthew 15 there is a story of a Canaanite, a Syrophoenician woman. "And behold, a woman of Canaan came from that region and cried out to Him, saying, 'Have mercy on me, O Lord, Son of David! My daughter is severely demon-possessed'" (Matthew 15:22).

Do you know what Jesus said to her? "He answered and said, 'I was not sent except to the lost sheep of the house of Israel. ...It is not good to take the children's bread and throw it to the little dogs'" (Matthew 15:24, 26).

Suppose Jesus talked to you that way. You would say, "Some caring Messiah! He called me a dog. He does not care about me and my daughter."

Do you know what that woman did? "She said, 'Yes, Lord, yet even the little dogs eat the crumbs which fall from their masters' table'" (Matthew 15:27). She was saying, "Lord, you described me perfectly. But I am a dog under Your table, and I'm going to stay there until I get a crumb from You."

Jesus' heart broke. He was not being cruel to that woman; He was trying to teach her to knock, to persist.

Then Jesus answered and said to her, "O woman, great is your faith! Let it be to you as you desire." And her daughter was healed from that very hour (Matthew 15:28).

Elijah was a prophet of God in the Old Testament. God had shut up Heaven, and for three years, it did not rain. The leaves were shriveled. The animals were dying. It was a judgment of God upon the land.

But then Elijah and the people prayed for rain for the glory of God. Elijah went up on the top of Mount Carmel. He sent his servant and said, "Go see if you see any clouds." The servant went. Nothing. Elijah prayed some more. He said, "Go again." Nothing. He prayed some more. "Go again."

On the seventh time, the servant came back and said, "I see a little cloud about the size of a man's hand."

Elijah said, "There is going to be an abundance of rain."

We need to keep on praying until God rains down upon us. Here was a man who knocked and kept on knocking, and that is what we need to do. If God does not answer your prayer, just keep on praying.

That brings up a question.

HOW LONG SHOULD WE CONTINUE TO PRAY?

This is how long you continue to pray: knock until you have the answer in your hand, or in your heart, or until God says, "No."

If you have the answer in the form of four tickets in your hand, you do not have to keep asking.

Or you might have the answer in your heart, when God says, "I have heard your prayer. Wait upon Me." I had a deep prayer request in my life one time which concerned some of my loved ones. I tried again to tell God how to do it, but He would not let me instruct Him. One day He said to me, "Adrian, trust Me. I am going to take care of it. I have heard your prayer." It took a while for that to come to me, but I had the answer in my heart.

Sometimes God will simply say, "No." Why? Because He does not love us? No—because He *does* love us. Three of God's greatest prophets in the Bible asked God to kill them. God said, "*No. I am not going to do that. That is not what you need.*"

You ask. You seek. You knock. The answer may be direct, or different, or delayed. But God answers prayer.

A WORSHIPING CHURCH

What is life's highest good? Is it service? That is wonderful. Is it sacrifice? Indeed, that is glorious. But Church, the bottom line of all of life—life's ultimate priority, highest good, supreme duty, and greatest privilege—is worship.

I want that to be riveted into your heart. This is not just rhetoric; I am talking about something that is transformational, that will change your Christian life from monotonous to momentous. Worship will free you and fulfill you, glorify God through you, and give you great joy. And the only way we can learn to worship as a church is to learn to worship as individuals.

In John 4, Jesus is on a journey. The Bible says, "He needed to go through Samaria" (John 4:4). That was not the easiest way; that was the mountainous way. If Jesus had wanted to take the easiest way, He would have gone down alongside the River Jordan. But Jesus "needed to go through Samaria."

The Samaritans were Jews who were left over from the exile, who then intermarried with the Canaanites. The Jews looked down on them as a mongrel race and had no dealings with them. The Samaritans were hostile to the Jews, and vice versa.

But now, Jesus is going through Samaria. It is the middle of the day. He is hot, tired, worn. He sits down on the curbing, the parapet around a well. The Bible says it was Jacob's well—a deep well, which is still there today. Jesus' disciples had gone into the city to buy some food.

A woman comes out there to the well. This woman was what we would call a shady lady. She had been married five times, and now she is living with a man without even the benefit of a marriage ceremony. She does not come out to draw water when the other women do, because those women would look down upon her, maybe even spit on her, so she comes out to the well by herself to draw water.

Jesus is there. He says to her: "Would you give Me a drink of water?"

> **Then the woman of Samaria said to Him, "How is it that You, being a Jew, ask a drink from me, a Samaritan woman?" For Jews have no dealings with Samaritans.**
> **Jesus answered and said to her, "If you knew the gift of God, and who it is who says to you, 'Give Me a drink,' you would have asked Him, and He would have given you living water."**
> **The woman said to Him, "Sir, You have nothing to draw with, and the well is deep. Where then do You get that living water?" (John 4:9-11).**

Jesus now begins to speak to this thirsty woman about real living water, a drink that would satisfy her forever and ever–because Jesus Christ is what every soul thirsts for. *He is the water of life.*

This poor woman is bound by sin. She has gone from husband to husband, deeper and deeper into sin. Not only that, but she is blinded by Satan. She does not know the way out.

Religion is a washout to her. It does not satisfy her hungry, thirsty soul. Broken by sorrow–think how pitiful this woman's life is! Jesus' heart goes out to her in compassion, as His heart goes out to you.

This woman needs to lift her eyes from the things of this Earth and learn how to worship. So, Jesus teaches her.

God is Spirit, and those who worship Him must worship in spirit and truth (John 4:24).

THE MEANING OF TRUE WORSHIP

This woman knew about worship, but she did not understand *true* worship. What she wants to do is argue about religion.

> *The woman said to Him, "Sir, I perceive that You are a prophet. Our fathers worshiped on this mountain, and you Jews say that in Jerusalem is the place where one ought to worship" (John 4:19-20).*

Remember, the Jews and the Samaritans were not getting along. Jesus said to her, "You worship what you do not know; we know what we worship, for salvation is of the Jews" (John 4:22). The Samaritans had rejected all of the Old Testament except for the five books of Moses. They were so certain that they knew the truth, that their worship was the right worship, and nobody else's worship was right. What they had was zeal and ignorance.

Today, too, the world is saturated with this. It is not that people do not worship. Oh yes, they have zeal, but it is *ignorant* worship. Do you know what a fanatic is? Somebody who has lost his direction and doubles his speed. That is what these Samaritans were doing.

What about the Jews? They had the truth, but they did not have any zeal. Jesus said to them, "Well did Isaiah prophesy of you hypocrites, as it is written: 'This people honors Me with their lips, but their heart is far from Me'" (Mark 7:6b).

Here you have enthusiastic heresy; there you have dead orthodoxy. Some fry in fanaticism. Some freeze in formalism, without the vitality of the Lord Jesus Christ.

The answer is not formalism *or* fanaticism; the answer is true worship. Not heat without light, nor light without heat, but true worship. It will be a great day in your life, and in the life of your church, when you stop enduring religion and start enjoying true worship. This is the highest good, the ultimate privilege: to worship God in spirit and in truth.

Look at the word "worship." It really comes from two words: *worth* and *ship*. Worship deals with worth. Show me how you worship, and I will tell you what God is worth to you. If your worship is not true worship, you have a low estimation of God. Worship goes beyond a church service. Worship goes beyond music. Worship goes beyond candles and incense.

Worship is all that we are, responding to all that God is, revealed in Jesus Christ.

You are going to worship something. Man is incurably religious. We have a God-shaped vacuum, and we are trying to fill it. If you do not worship the true God, you are going to worship in dead orthodoxy, or ignorant zeal, or you will worship some idol.

Anything you love more, fear more, and serve more than the Almighty is your idol. It may be a movie star. It may be a sports idol. It may be money. It may be pleasure. It may be illicit sex. It may be the Super Bowl. For some people, that is a no-brainer: if they had to choose between the Super Bowl and church, they would choose the Super Bowl. There is no greater sin than idolatry.

If you do not practice true worship, you will find a substitute for worship, because nature abhors a vacuum. Today, you can go into what is called a house of worship and find people lighting candles, bowing down, and kissing images. They call that worship.

Ask them, "Why do you have those images?"

They will say, "They remind us of the one true God."

Suppose a woman walks into a room and finds her husband embracing another woman, and he says, "Now, wait a minute, sweetheart. Don't get the wrong idea. She just reminds me so much of you." Graven images are no substitute for true worship!

"God is Spirit, and those who worship Him must worship in spirit and truth" (John 4:24). There is no image, no likeness, that you can use as a substitute for God. "'To whom then will you liken Me, or to whom shall I be equal?' says the Holy One" (Isaiah 40:25).

THE MOTIVE OF TRUE WORSHIP

> *"But the hour is coming, and now is, when the true worshipers will worship the Father in spirit and truth; for the Father is seeking such to worship Him"* (John 4:23).

Why should you worship? Because that is what God wants of you. The Father seeks that for two major reasons.

WHAT WORSHIP DOES FOR THE WORSHIPER

This is the reason idolatry is such a sin: first the man molds the idol, and then the idol molds the man. We become like what we worship.

That is true in the negative sense, and it is also true in the positive sense. The more you worship God, the more you will become like God.

If you leave an iron poker in the fire, before long, the fire will be in the poker. When you worship God, it is not very long until God's fire will be in you. "But we all, with unveiled face, beholding as in a mirror the glory of the Lord, are being transformed into the same image from glory to glory, just as by the Spirit of the Lord" (2 Corinthians 3:18). As you contemplate the Lord, as you worship the Lord, as you keep your heart open to the Lord, you will be changed to be more and more like the Lord Jesus Christ.

Do other people see Jesus in you? Do not answer rhetorically. Answer sincerely in your heart. Are you being changed day by day by day into the glory of our Lord and Savior Jesus Christ?

To spend time with God, worshiping, will make you godly. We become like the things with which we spend time. They say that even a husband and wife begin to look like each other. So why do we worship? Because of what worship does for us.

WHAT GOD DESIRES FROM US

God desires worship for Himself. The need for worship is rooted in the very nature of God. Do not miss this: "The Father is seeking such to worship Him."

"Father" is not what God is like; "Father" is what God *is*. Feminists try to talk about a "mother god." That is absolute, unmitigated gall and ignorance. God is Father! We do not get our idea of God from fatherhood; we get an idea of fatherhood from God. If you take away the Fatherhood of God, you miss the Bible. Jesus' favorite term for the Almighty is, "Father." He used it more than 70 times in Scripture.

There are things about God that you will never understand. I do not even know if we will understand them when we get to glory. God's omnipotence—His limitless power. God's omniscience—He knows everything. God's omnipresence—He is everywhere. God's eternality—He never had a beginning and never has an ending. Those are concepts beyond the human mind, but you do not have to understand them to know and love God.

When I was a little boy, four or five years old, I would see my daddy all dressed up to go off to work, with his little valise that he kept his papers in. I would see him kiss my mother goodbye, and he would go off. I would watch him leave. I had no idea what he did, what his job was. But I will tell you one thing: I knew my daddy!

You do not have to understand all the intricacies of Almighty God. You do not have to understand how He keeps the sun, moon, and stars in orbit to call Him Father, if you have been born again.

Worship is rooted in the Fatherhood of God. What did my father want from me? He did not want me to understand his profession; he wanted me to love him. When we worship, we are just responding to the Father's love. I love my Father because He first loved me.

There is something about a father's heart that wants the love of his children.

Once, we had a father-daughter banquet at church. All those beautiful little girls dressed up with their daddies—it was wonderful. My daughter Janice and I were there. Janice stood up first and spoke of what her father meant to her. I could not tell you how my heart was blessed, how deeply moved, and how grateful I was to hear my child speak, not only privately to me, but openly and publicly, of her love and her devotion to her father.

Friend, that is the way God's great heart is. God wants us to worship, first, because worship changes us, but also because of what worship does for God: it gives Him pleasure.

Every Father's Day, little children wonder, "What can I get for Daddy?" You could give him some slippers or a necktie, but do you know what your daddy wants? Love!

What can you give to God today? You think, "I can't sing like these other people. I can't preach like so-and-so." There is nobody who can love God better than you can, and that is what God wants more than anything else.

THE METHOD OF TRUE WORSHIP

Jesus said we are to worship in spirit. He is not talking about the Holy Spirit. He is talking about the human spirit. That is, worship comes out of the inner man. "For God is my witness, whom I serve with my spirit" (Romans 1:9a).

Now, the human spirit cannot worship unless it is enjoined with the Holy Spirit, but God the Holy Spirit comes into the human spirit to help us to worship. That is the reason you must be saved and Spirit-filled to truly worship.

If you are having trouble worshiping, may I tell you what your problem is? Your spirit.

My wife, Joyce, had a brother who was sort of a flirt. Joyce and I prayed and prayed for him. Every now and then, he would grudgingly come to hear me preach.

Then he got saved. He got saved and a half. Radically, dramatically. He came to hear me preach again, and he said, "Adrian, boy, that's great. You don't preach like you used to!"

I said, "I preach the same way I have been preaching. You don't hear like you used to."

When you get your heart right, a church service is not going to be boring. You have never been in a boring worship service; there is no such thing. You worship in spirit, and then you worship in truth.

Worship that is not built on truth is not true worship. Worship built on truth goes beyond spirit, beyond subjectivism.

"The Lord is near to all who call upon Him, to all who call upon Him in truth" (Psalm 145:18).

Your worship of God will never rise above your knowledge, based on truth. That is why there should always be exposition of truth from the pulpit. You cannot worship God ignorantly. Jesus told this Samaritan woman, "You worship what you do not know" (John 4:22a). Worship is a loving response to the God revealed in the Bible. That is why we study the Bible.

Some people say, "Are we going to have a Bible study today, or a worship service?" Yes! They think that when we sing and pray and praise and fellowship, that is worship. But the preaching of the Word of God is worship. We worship God *in truth*, and if we do not, the Church becomes syrupy. It becomes subjective rather than objective.

"For God is the King of all the earth; *sing* praises with *understanding*" (Psalm 47:7, emphasis added). That is spirit and that is truth. If you have all emotionalism, you blow up. If you have all truth, you dry up. But if you have spirit and truth, you grow up.

Jesus gave us the great commandment, and it deals with worship.

> **"And you shall love the Lord your God with all your heart, with all your soul, with all your mind, and with all your strength." This is the first commandment (Mark 12:30).**

Remember: what is the highest good? What is the bottom line? What is the ultimate privilege? Here, Jesus is saying it so clearly: we are to love God.

How are we going to love Him? Write down four words and put them in your purse, your pocketbook, or your shirt pocket, and carry them with you.

Love your God passionately—with as much as is in you. Half-hearted worship is an insult to Almighty God.

Love God selflessly—with all your soul. The soul is the self. You are self-centered by nature. You may have heard somebody say, "Well, I came to church, and I didn't get anything out of it." Who said you were supposed to get anything out of it? Ask yourself this question: *Did God receive anything from my worship? Did God get something out of it?* We are here to glorify God. When you take your mind off yourself and put your mind on God, and stop saying, "What am I going to get?" and begin to say, "What am I going to give?," the church is transformed into a worshiping church.

Love Him thoughtfully—with all your heart. A full heart is no excuse for an empty head. Serve the Lord with knowledge and wisdom. Love Him in spirit and in truth.

Love Him practically—with all your strength. "And whatever you do in word or deed, do all in the name of the Lord Jesus, giving thanks to God the Father through Him" (Colossians 3:17).

What is worship? It is giving God glory. You can change the place where you go to work tomorrow morning if you just change your boss. You do not work for that man; you work for God. "Bondservants, be obedient to those who are your masters according to the flesh, with fear and trembling, in sincerity of heart, as to Christ" (Ephesians 6:5). Your workplace can be your temple of devotion, your lampstand of witness, as you worship God with all your strength.

That is what Jesus was telling this Samaritan woman.

She said, "Do we worship here, or do we worship there?"

Jesus said, "You worship in spirit and in truth." There is no place that is not a holy place. There is no ground that is not sacred. There is no time that should not be a time of worship. So, when we come to church, we do not come merely to worship; we bring our worship to church. When you come in with a heart aflame, when you come in hardly waiting to sing, to fellowship, to study the Word of God, then your church becomes a worshiping church.

That will make the Church what God desires her to be.

A CONQUERING CHURCH

When God made you, He designed you for mastery. You were not designed to fail. You were designed to have dominion. When you were born again, you were born to win. Here is one purpose for which God made you:

Then God said, "Let Us make man in Our image, according to Our likeness; let them have dominion over the fish of the sea, over the birds of the air, and over the cattle, over all the earth and over every creeping thing that creeps on the earth" (Genesis 1:26).

If black print on white paper means anything, that means that Man—as God designed him and created him—was given rule, to control and master the Earth and its resources. Man was to be king of the Earth. "You have made him to have dominion over the works of Your hands; You have put all things under his feet" (Psalm 8:6).

Well, look at today's news. It is obvious that Man does not have dominion. All things are not under his feet. There is death, disease, hate, war, crime, lust, sorrow, disappointment, despair—everywhere. Yet Man is supposed to have dominion. Something has gone wrong.

Thank God, He has done something about it.

MAN LEGALLY LOST DOMINION

This dominion Man was supposed to have, and was given, was legally lost by Adam. Key words: *legally*, and *Adam*.

Had there been no Adam, there would have been no you. You are connected to Adam. You might say, "I don't believe people ought to be lost because of one man." Well, you ought to be glad that a person can be lost by one man, because also a person can be saved by one man.

But what happened?

God describes us this way:

And you He made alive, who were dead in trespasses and sins, in which you once walked according to the course of this world, according to the prince of the power of the air, the spirit who now works in the sons of disobedience... (Ephesians 2:1-2).

Who is "the prince of the power of the air"? Who is the spirit who works in the disobedient? The devil himself.

God did not create a devil. God created a perfect being, but He gave that perfect being the power of choice, and Satan chose to rebel against God. Satan's original name was *Lucifer*, which means "light bearer." *Satan* means "adversary." The bearer of light became the master of darkness.

What happened is this: Satan had pride in his heart. He thought to himself, "I am too great, too wise, too wonderful to be anything less than God."

For you have said in your heart: "I will ascend into heaven, I will exalt my throne above the stars of God;

> *I will also sit on the mount of the congregation on the farthest sides of the north..."* (Isaiah 14:13).

But no sooner had Satan unsheathed his sword of rebellion than the thunders of God rolled down through the corridors of Heaven, and Satan was banished.

The rebellion that would not work in Heaven, was turned to Earth. Satan now turned his attention to Man. Satan came to this Earth to enthrone himself in the heart and mind of Man.

The entire Universe is run by laws—God's laws. God created these laws, and God keeps these laws.

When God gave Adam dominion, it was a legal gift. If I give something to you, it is yours. You become the legal possessor of it. Once I give it to you, you are free to do with it as you will.

God legally gave Adam dominion. Adam forfeited dominion to Satan.

I had a friend in college whose father gave him a brand-new car. Do you know what my friend did? He gave it away to another student. If you were that boy's father, what would you say, what would you think, what would you do? I will tell you one thing: that father could not go and take it away from that student. The dad gave it to his son, and his son gave it to another. It was legally given. It was legally lost.

Adam willfully turned over his dominion when he chose to obey Satan and ate of the forbidden fruit. Adam yielded himself to Satan and became the servant of Satan.

> **Do you not know that to whom you present yourselves slaves to obey, you are that one's slaves whom you obey, whether of sin leading to death, or of obedience leading to righteousness? (Romans 6:16).**

In Luke 4, the devil tempted Jesus. He took Jesus up to a high mountain and showed Him the kingdoms of the world in a moment. And Satan said this to the Son of God: "All this authority I will give You, and their glory; for this has been delivered to me, and I give it to whomever I wish. Therefore, if You will worship before me, all will be Yours" (Luke 4:6b-7).

Satan has always wanted to be worshiped. But the point in this passage is: "this has been delivered to me." When Adam, who was made for dominion, turned it over to Satan, he lost all his legal rights and Satan became the legal possessor of Adam's dominion. Now Adam is spiritually dead and legally dethroned.

The Apostle Paul talks about the mayhem, the disillusionment, the deadness, and the darkness that is in the hearts and minds of men—and he says they are those "whose minds the god of this age has blinded, who do not believe" (2 Corinthians 4:4a).

Who is the god of this world? Satan. No wonder the Bible says, "We do not wrestle against flesh and blood, but against principalities, against powers, against the rulers of the darkness of this age, against spiritual hosts of wickedness in the heavenly places" (Ephesians 6:12).

JESUS RIGHTFULLY RECOVERED DOMINION

We are talking about a conquering Church. This dominion that was legally lost by Adam has been rightfully recovered by Jesus.

The word "rightfully" is very important. Jesus did not just walk in and kick Satan out. He did not say, "I don't care what Adam did; I'm taking it back." Dominion legally lost must be legally regained.

In Ephesians 1, Paul is praying:

...That the God of our Lord Jesus Christ, the Father of glory, may give to you the spirit of wisdom and revelation in the knowledge of Him, the eyes of your understanding being enlightened; that you may know *what is the hope of His calling, what are the riches of the glory of His inheritance in the saints, and what is the exceeding greatness of His power toward us who believe, according to the working of His mighty power which He worked in Christ when He raised Him from the dead and seated Him at His right hand in the heavenly places, far above all principality and power and might and dominion, and every name that is named, not only in this age but also in that which is to come* (Ephesians 1:17-21, emphasis added).

What does all that mean? Paul is praying, "Oh God, open their eyes. Help them to understand that when Jesus died, rose again, and ascended to the high hills of glory, He decimated Satan's kingdom, and He is above all powers and principalities."

Remember that Paul says in Ephesians 6:12 that we wrestle against principalities and powers. Here, he is saying that Jesus is high above all those things. What was legally lost in Adam was rightfully and righteously regained in Christ through His death, burial, and resurrection.

But suppose God had just stepped in, and said, "I am God. Out of here, Satan! I'm going to go back to the beginning, to start all over again." As God, He could do whatever He wanted. But He would have broken His own law.

Law would have become a farce if God had failed to keep His own law.

God owes the devil nothing at all, but God owes something to His own righteousness, to His own principle of justice. If God had overlooked the legality in this matter, then God Himself would have participated in illegality. God would have had to admit that sin had ultimately won. Even if God had stepped in by divine power and set Satan aside, the law still would have been there. So, what was God going to do?

Dominion was lost by a man. It must be legally recovered by a man.

There is no member of Adam's race that can be found who could undo what Adam did—because all of us are the sons of Adam. "In Adam all die" (1 Corinthians 15:22a). When he obeyed Satan, Adam did not enthrone himself; he enthroned Satan. Adam, therefore, became a slave of Satan. The sons of slaves are slaves themselves because the master owns the slave and all his children. So, there are none among the sons of men who can redeem us, because we are all slaves.

Yet dominion must be redeemed by a man. God's answer is found in Jesus Christ, the Son of God, who stepped out of Heaven and Himself became a man. God defeated Satan with the second Adam.

> **For since by man came death, by Man also came the resurrection of the dead. For as in Adam all die, even so in Christ all shall be made alive (1 Corinthians 15:21-22).**

We are flesh and blood. Jesus took upon Himself flesh and blood. "Inasmuch then as the children have partaken of flesh and blood, He Himself likewise shared in the same, that through death He might destroy him who had the power of death, that is, the devil" (Hebrews 2:14). Jesus became a man so that He could die and destroy Satan at Calvary. The full penalty of sin was paid. Satan's contract was annulled, and Satan's back was broken.

> *Even so we, when we were children, were in bondage under the elements of the world. But when the fullness of the time had come, God sent forth His Son, born of a woman, born under the law, to redeem those who were under the law, that we might receive the adoption as sons (Galatians 4:3-5).*

God did it all legally. This is the reason for Christmas. This is the reason the Son of God, who had always existed in the bosom of the Father, stepped out of the glory of Heaven, and came down to this wicked, sinful Earth, and became a man through a virgin's womb. By a man dominion was lost, by a man it must be recovered; so, God became a man.

JESUS, THE LAST ADAM

Jesus, the Son of God, was different from every other man that Satan had ever dealt with, except for Adam. This difference was that Jesus was sinless. So was Adam—at first.

Jesus, born of a virgin, inherited none of Adam's sin. Jesus is not the son of Adam; He is the Son of God. He was not born a slave.

He was God of very God. This is not taking away from His deity but reminding us of His humanity. He had *always* been deity, but He *became* human so that He might legally take back our lost estate.

Suppose Jesus, as God, were to decimate Satan and say, "Satan, be gone to the pit! I'm taking it all back." What kind of an example could He be to me? I am not God. No—Jesus could have defeated Satan as very God of very God, but He is defeating Satan as very man of very man.

When Satan sees Jesus now on the scene, he knows he must have another battle. He must defeat the last Adam as he defeated the first Adam. He must get the second Adam to sin as he got the first one to sin.

We see the battle ensue in Luke 4.

IN THE WILDERNESS

Jesus, filled with the Holy Spirit, begins His public ministry by going out into the wilderness to fast for forty days and forty nights. "And in those days He ate nothing, and afterward, when they had ended, He was hungry" (Luke 4:2b). That is probably the greatest understatement in the Bible.

At that time Satan came to Him, thinking, "He is weakened. I can overcome Him."

> **And the devil said to Him, "If You are the Son of God, command this stone to become bread."**
>
> **But Jesus answered him, saying, "It is written, 'Man shall not live by bread alone, but by every word of God'" (Luke 4:3-4).**

Notice that "*if* You are the Son of God..." What a sneer. But Jesus uses the sword of the Spirit, the Word of God, and runs Satan through.

Satan staggers back up again.

> **Then the devil, taking Him up on a high mountain, showed Him all the kingdoms of the world in a moment**

> of time. And the devil said to Him, "All this authority I will give You, and their glory; for this has been delivered to me, and I give it to whomever I wish. Therefore, if You will worship before me, all will be Yours."
>
> And Jesus answered and said to him, "Get behind Me, Satan! For it is written, 'You shall worship the LORD your God, and Him only you shall serve'" (Luke 4:5-8).

Jesus runs him through again. Satan recoils and comes back one more time.

> **Then he brought Him to Jerusalem, set Him on the pinnacle of the temple, and said to Him, "If You are the Son of God, throw Yourself down from here. For it is written: 'He shall give His angels charge over you, to keep you,' and, 'In their hands they shall bear you up, lest you dash your foot against a stone.'"**
>
> And Jesus answered and said to him, "It has been said, 'You shall not tempt the LORD your God'" (Luke 4:9-12).

The thing I want you to understand is that Jesus used the same weapons that Adam had: the Word of God and the Spirit of God. Jesus did not pull rank on Adam. What Adam lost in the Garden, Jesus overcame in a wilderness.

Satan withdraws for a while, the Bible says, "until an opportune time" (Luke 4:13b). That opportune time came at dark Gethsemane.

IN GETHSEMANE

Jesus, knowing that He was facing the cross, went to pray. The Bible calls it an "agony." Agon was the Greek word for a place of warfare, battle, or contest. This was agony.

Jesus is there praying with His face on the ground. His sweat becomes blood and mingles with the black dirt. "He went a little farther and fell on His face, and prayed, saying, 'O My Father, if it is possible, let this cup pass from Me'" (Matthew 26:39a).

What was in that cup? Your sin. My sin. Our sin. The sin of all the world that ever will be. Every rape, every murder, every brutality, every blasphemy, every sexual perversion was in that cup. "He made Him who knew no sin to be sin for us, that we might become the righteousness of God in Him" (2 Corinthians 5:21). Jesus never sinned, but He had to take our sin upon Himself. He took that bitter cup and said, "Nevertheless, not as I will, but as You will" (Matthew 26:39b).

You say, "Well, He was God." Yes, but He was Man also. As a man, He was saying, "O God, I don't want to do this." Does it bother you that Jesus shrank from the cross? I am glad He did because it shows His humanity. He did not swagger up to the cross and say, "I am God. This can't hurt Me." Oh, the agony! Father, let it pass; *nevertheless…*

Friend, your destiny hangs on that word. *Nevertheless.* Satan was defeated again.

He was still looking for a more opportune time. The hounds of Hell are baying after the Lord, driving Him to Calvary. Satan has the idea that perhaps, when faced with the cross, Jesus will turn away from the battle. The demonic pressure is indescribable.

Jesus could have stepped out of the whole thing and said, "That's enough." They said of Him when He was on the cross, "He saved others; Himself He cannot save" (Mark 15:31b). Wrong! Himself He *would not* save! He was not held to the cross by those searing nails, but by the golden bonds of love.

Jesus Christ went to bloody Calvary. He bowed His head and said, "It is finished!" That means *it is paid in full.* All of

Satan's legal claims are now nullified. What was lost by a man is regained by a man. Legally lost, legally regained.

But it is not over yet. After the death there is the glorious resurrection. After the resurrection, there is the magnificent ascension. After the ascension, there is the enthronement of our Lord and Savior Jesus Christ.

DOMINION IS GIVEN TO THE CHURCH

Dominion is now gloriously given to the Church. If you do not understand this, then you do not understand what Paul was praying: "…That you may know what is the hope of His calling, what are the riches of the glory of His inheritance in the saints" (Ephesians 1:18b).

One demon said to another demon, "If those liberal theologians ever really admit that Jesus has been raised from the dead and ascended and is over all, Hell help me; all Heaven will break loose!"

Jesus is now…

> *…far above all principality and power and might and dominion, and every name that is named, not only in this age but also in that which is to come. And He put all things under His feet, and gave Him to be head over all things to the church, which is His body, the fullness of Him who fills all in all (Ephesians 1:21-23).*

Paul is talking about us, now. The Church is Christ's body. The Church is not an organization with Jesus as the president; it is an organism with Jesus as the Head.

We are one with the Lord Jesus. He took our sins that we

might take His innocence. He took our guilt that we might be acquitted. He took our despair that we might have His joy, our shame that we might know His glory, the pains of Hell that we might know the glories of Heaven. We are now in Him.

He says to us as He sends us out, "All authority has been given to Me in heaven and on earth. Go therefore" (Matthew 28:18b-19a).

Does Jesus have authority over Satan? Yes. So do you. Does Jesus have constant victory? Yes. So do you. Satan hopes that you never learn this lesson: that Christ has given you authority over all the power of the enemy.

The dominion that Adam lost was won back by Christ and given to the Church! Would to God that we could understand this! The Lamb has prevailed. His conquest is complete. He conquered on the tree and in the tomb, and now He sits upon the throne.

The Bible says God has, "raised us up together, and made us sit together in the heavenly places in Christ Jesus" (Ephesians 2:6). Most people say, "Keep looking up." We look down. All things are under Christ's feet; therefore, they are under our feet.

You think, "Why then is my life so miserable, so defeated?" Because you fail to understand and put into practice what I have just preached. God's plan for you, for your church, for the Church, is constant, continual, conspicuous victory.

Satan has no power over you—none. Do not say, "The devil made me do it." He can't. The only power Satan has over you is what you yield to him by unbelief.

Science cannot explain it, history cannot repeat it, and time will never blot it out. Thank God for our victory!

A BIBLE-BELIEVING CHURCH

I do not have enough vocabulary to tell you how important it is for your faith to rest in the Word of God.

What I want you to see is what Jesus thought of His Bible, for the servant must be like his master.

Only ignorance scoffs at the fact that Jesus Christ was a historical character; we know that beyond the shadow of any doubt. But just who was this Jesus? Scholars are still scratching their heads and thinking. We know, because we have a Bible. Jesus authenticates the Bible, and the Bible authenticates Jesus. They rise or fall together.

Jesus was here on Earth before the New Testament was ever written. He said,

> **"Do not think that I came to destroy the Law or the Prophets. I did not come to destroy but to fulfill. For assuredly, I say to you, till heaven and earth pass away, one jot or one tittle will by no means pass from the law till all is fulfilled" (Matthew 5:17-18).**

"The Law and the Prophets" was what the Jews called, and still call, the Old Testament. A jot is the smallest letter in the Greek alphabet, which we call an *iota*. A *tittle* is the smallest punctuation mark, almost like a fly speck. Jesus is saying, "This thing is so inspired that the smallest, most minute punctuations marks will never fail."

The Church is, and must always be, a Bible-based Church.

JESUS FULFILLS OLD TESTAMENT PROPHECY

The Old Testament is a book of prophecy, and it predicts the Lord Jesus Christ. "I did not come to destroy, but to fulfill." Do you want a key to understanding the Bible? Look for Jesus in it. If you read the Bible and do not find Jesus, re-read. The Bible has one hero, Jesus; one villain, Satan; one problem, sin; and one solution, salvation.

Let me point out what I am talking about when I say that Jesus and the Bible rise or stand together.

"And beginning at Moses and all the Prophets, He expounded to them in all the Scriptures the things concerning Himself" (Luke 24:27). That is, Jesus took the Old Testament and started with Moses (Genesis, Exodus, Leviticus, Numbers, and Deuteronomy) and went on to the Prophets.

People say, "Have you read the four Gospels?" I have read all 66. They are all about the Lord Jesus Christ. If you are reading the lists of names in Genesis that sound like a Hebrew telephone directory, you may say, "Where is Jesus there?" But if you understand Bible history, you will understand that ultimately it is all written to present the Lord Jesus Christ.

"To Him [Jesus] all the prophets witness that, through His name, whoever believes in Him will receive remission of sins" (Acts 10:43, word in brackets added). Do not get the idea that the Old Testament was written about one thing and the New Testament was written about something else. The Savior, and the salvation that the Savior provides, are presented in the Old Testament.

Jesus said, "You search the Scriptures, for in them you think you have eternal life; and these are they which testify of Me" (John 5:39). I remind you that the Bible of Jesus' day was the Old Testament. He says, "These testify of Me."

God has no program, no plans, no purposes that do not ultimately center on the Lord Jesus Christ. Jesus is in all of the Bible, and you will find Him especially in the prophecy.

Jesus Christ is the only person ever born to this world whose ancestry, place and manner of birth, infancy, forerunner, manhood, teaching, character, preaching, reception, rejection, death, burial, resurrection, and ascension were all prophesied centuries before He was born.

In the Old Testament there are 333 precise prophecies concerning Jesus Christ. Professor Peter Stoner at Westmont College looked at only eight of these, to determine the possibility of them being fulfilled by chance. He wrote:

> We find that the chance that any man might have lived down to the present time and fulfilled all eight prophecies is 1 in 10 to the 17th power.

That is 1 in 100,000,000,000,000,000. Stoner goes on to illustrate this:

> Suppose that we take 10 to the 17th power in silver dollars and lay them on the face of Texas. They will cover all of the state two feet deep. Now mark one of these silver dollars and stir the whole mass thoroughly, all over the state. Blindfold a man and tell him that he can travel as

far as he wishes, but he must pick up one silver dollar and say that this is the right one. What chance would he have of getting the right one? Just the same chance that the prophets would have had of writing these eight prophecies and having them all come true in any one man, from their day to the present time, providing they wrote using their own wisdom.

And he is only dealing with eight of these 333 Old Testament prophecies. When you add them up, the possibility of chance greatly diminishes.

My wife and I have a son who lives in Spain. When I want to call David, I pick up the phone and dial a specific number, and he is on the other end. But think how the mathematical situation works out.

When I pick up the phone, I eliminate everybody who does not have a telephone. When I dial the overseas operator or number, I know that I am not going to talk to anybody in North America. Hundreds of millions of people are cut out of the equation now. Then I dial the country's number, and we eliminate the billions of people who live in other countries. I dial the area code. Then I begin to dial David's personal number. The first digit eliminates everybody whose number does not begin with that digit. Then the second digit, and so on, and we keep narrowing the scope until the phone rings and I hear the voice I love to hear.

Do you think someone could pick up a telephone and just dial numbers at random and reach his loved one? No! It is a mathematical impossibility.

When we are looking for Jesus Christ, we are looking for someone from the human race. You say, "I thought Jesus was God." He is God, but He is also human. Genesis 3:15 is the first prophecy we have which says that He is a man, not an angel or some other creature. "I will put enmity between you and the woman, and between your seed and her Seed" (Genesis 3:15a).

Then we dial someone who is from a section of that human race. Three sections came out of the ark: Ham, Shem, and Japheth. "Blessed be the Lord, the God of Shem" (Genesis 9:26b). So, Jesus must be a Semite, or Shemite.

Now we tighten the focus, and we have a nation from the Semites. God said to Abraham that He would make him into a great nation. "In your seed all the nations of the earth shall be blessed" (Genesis 22:18a). That is, Messiah was going to come through Abraham.

But then out of that nation was going to come a tribe. "The scepter shall not depart from Judah, nor a lawgiver from between his feet, until Shiloh comes; and to Him shall be the obedience of the people" (Genesis 49:10).

Narrow it just a bit more: there is a family of that tribe from whom Messiah will come. In 1 Samuel 16, we find out a man named Jesse has a son named David, who will be the progenitor according to the flesh of the Savior of the world.

Now we notice that there is a specific woman of that family who will give birth to the Messiah. "Behold, the virgin shall conceive and bear a Son, and shall call His name Immanuel" (Isaiah 7:14b).

Then we find out that there is a Son, born of that woman, of that family, of that tribe, of that nation, of that race. Hello, Jesus!

Do you think for one minute that this happened by chance?

Some people today tell us, "The Bible is inspired in spots." They think they are inspired to be able to spot the spots. But if you cannot trust all of it as God originally gave it, then you cannot trust any of it.

The Bible is inspired in two ways.

The Bible is verbally inspired. Verba in Latin means "word." That means not just the thoughts, but the words are inspired. Jesus said, "Man shall not live by bread alone, but by every word that proceeds from the mouth of God" (Matthew 4:4b). You cannot have thoughts without words any more than you could have mathematics without numbers.

The Bible is also plenarily inspired. That means full, all of it—Genesis to Revelation. Do not ever slip on this. As you go out, people are going to plant doubt in your mind with their verbal gymnastics. Anybody who puts doubt in your mind concerning the Word of God is doing the work of the devil. Students, get a grip on the Word of God.

Your view of the Bible had better be the view your Savior had, who said, "One jot or one tittle will by no means pass from the law till all is fulfilled" (Matthew 5:18b). If that is not true, you can only have one of two conclusions: either Jesus was so ignorant that He did not know the Bible was not true, or Jesus knew it, but He was so dishonest that He would not admit it.

Your savior may be ignorant or dishonest, but my Savior is not.

JESUS FULFILLS THE PURPOSE OF THE LAW

What is the purpose of the Old Testament Law?

The Bible teaches that the Law is a schoolmaster to bring us to Christ. The Law cannot save us. All it does is show us our need for the dear Savior. "For Christ is the end of the law for righteousness to everyone who believes" (Romans 10:4).

When you think of the Law, think of the Ten Commandments, because they summarize the Law. Jesus did not come to say that the Ten Commandments do not matter anymore. He came to fulfill the Law. When you understand this, you understand what the cross is about. When Jesus Christ died, He bowed His head and said, "It is finished!" *I have fulfilled it. I have met every demand of the Law.*

If Jesus had not met every demand of the Law, He could not be your Savior. God demanded a perfect, sinless sacrifice, born of a virgin, with none of the Adamic nature in Him. Jesus Christ met every standard, every requirement of the law of God. Had Jesus not fulfilled the righteousness of the law, you and I could never be righteous. Jesus fulfilled the Law for us that grace might fulfill it in us.

The Law says, "Do this and you will live."

The Gospel says, "Live and you will do."

The Law says, "Pay me what you owe."

The Gospel says, "I forgive all."

The Law says, "You shall love the Lord your God with all your heart, with all your soul, and with all your strength" (Deuteronomy 6:5).

The Gospel says, "In this is love, not that we loved God, but that He loved us and sent His Son to be the propitiation for our sins" (1 John 4:10).

The Law says, "'Cursed is the one who does not confirm all the words of this law by observing them.' And all the people shall say, 'Amen!'" (Deuteronomy 27:26).

The Gospel says, "Blessed are those whose lawless deeds are forgiven, and whose sins are covered" (Romans 4:7).

The Law says, "For the wages of sin is death…" (Romans 6:23a).

The Gospel says "...But the gift of God is eternal life in Christ Jesus our Lord" (Romans 6:23b).

The Law says, "Do."

The Gospel says, "Done."

JESUS FULFILLS THE PROMISED PROVISION

The Law is here to tell us that we are sinners, that we are lost. We cannot save ourselves.

You might say, "My religion is the Ten Commandments." Then you are going to die and go to Hell. "That's blunt..." I meant it to be.

"For whoever shall keep the whole law, and yet stumble in one point, he is guilty of all" (James 2:10). Is there anybody who would have the audacity, the unmitigated gall to stand and say, "I have never broken one of the Ten Commandments"? Of course not!

If you have broken one of the commandments, you have broken them all in spirit. The Law is a unit, and God does not grade on the curve. Imagine yourself hanging over a furnace of fire, suspended by a chain. Nine links in that chain are made of forged steel, and one link is made of crepe paper. How safe are you?

I am a sinner. You are a sinner. Jesus came to save sinners. He suffered, bled, and died on that cross, and paid every debt we owe. He fulfilled the purpose of the Law, which is to bring us to Christ. We cannot save ourselves, but Jesus died to save us. That is the Gospel. The Gospel, friend, is good news.

"Does that mean, then, that it doesn't matter how I live? Are the Ten Commandments obsolete?" No, they are absolute.

Every day of your life you should want to live by God's blessed commandments.

The Bible says, "the righteous requirement of the law might be fulfilled in us who do not walk according to the flesh but according to the Spirit" (Romans 8:4). You cannot do that without Jesus Christ in you.

A CARING CHURCH

On September 12, 1931, a baby boy named Adrian was born at the Good Samaritan Hospital. That hospital was named for a particular story in Luke 10.

Other than the story of the prodigal son, this is probably the best-known, best-loved parable of our Lord and Savior Jesus Christ. But it is important that we get the background so that we can really understand it.

> **Behold, a certain lawyer stood up and tested Him, saying, "Teacher, what shall I do to inherit eternal life?" (Luke 10:25).**

This was a dishonest question from a crooked lawyer. Jesus always answered a dishonest question with another question. "He said to him, 'What is written in the law? What is your reading of it?'" (Luke 10:26).

Remember that Jesus came to fulfill the Law. He is going to show this lawyer how much he is lacking.

The crooked lawyer was a smart man, because he gave the right answer, from the book of Deuteronomy. "So he answered and said, 'You shall love the Lord your God with all your heart, with all your soul, with all your strength, and with all your mind,' and 'your neighbor as yourself.' And He [Jesus] said to him, 'You have answered rightly; do this and you will live'" (Luke 10:27-28, word in brackets added).

That is, "Young man, you think you can keep the Law? Keep it and you will live." Of course, he could not keep it. Jesus knew he *did* not keep it.

This man had a clear grasp of the demands of the Law in the Old Testament. He had studied Deuteronomy, Leviticus, and so on, and he had crystallized the whole thing. He had religion, but he had no reality. He was right, but dead right. There is nothing deader than dead orthodoxy—people who have their doctrine embalmed and pickled.

If your congregation is like any congregation, there are a great number of people in it who have their head knowledge, but do not know Christ.

When the wise men came in Matthew 2, Herod wanted to know where Jesus was to be born. "And he sent them to Bethlehem and said, 'Go and search carefully for the young Child, and when you have found Him, bring back word to me, that I may come and worship Him also'" (Matthew 2:8b). Lying rascal. He wanted to obliterate Jesus.

But whom did he ask? The scribes. They told him correctly where Messiah was to be born—but they themselves did not go. Is that not strange? They had the knowledge. They had a creed, but they did not have Christ.

Sometimes I talk to people and say, "Are you saved?" and they say, "Oh, yes, I know the plan of salvation." You are not saved by the plan of salvation. You are saved by the Man of salvation.

This lawyer in Luke 10 was smart, but dishonest. "But he, wanting to justify himself, said to Jesus, 'And who is my neighbor?'" (Luke 10:29). He did not want to love anybody he did not have to. He wanted to close the circle a little bit.

Notice that the answer he gave just before this is that you are to love God with all of your being and love your neighbor as yourself. (See Luke 10:27, above.) This lawyer did not ask anything about loving God. Why? Because that is private and secret. No one could see his heart. But whether or not he loved his neighbor was something that *could* be seen.

Jesus told him this story.

THE PARABLE OF THE GOOD SAMARITAN

Then Jesus answered and said:

> "A certain man went down from Jerusalem to Jericho, and fell among thieves, who stripped him of his clothing, wounded him, and departed, leaving him half dead. Now by chance a certain priest came down that road. And when he saw him, he passed by on the other side. Likewise a Levite, when he arrived at the place, came and looked, and passed by on the other side. But a certain Samaritan, as he journeyed, came where he was. And when he saw him, he had compassion. So he went to him and bandaged his wounds, pouring on oil and wine; and he set him on his own animal, brought him to an inn, and took care of him. On the next day, when he departed, he took out two denarii, gave them to the innkeeper, and said to him, 'Take care of him; and whatever more you spend, when I come again, I will repay you.' So which of these three do you think was neighbor to him who fell among the thieves?" And he said, "He who showed mercy on him."
>
> Then Jesus said to him, "Go and do likewise" (Luke 10:30-37).

When I study the Bible, I always marvel at the wisdom of Jesus Christ. Every parable that Jesus told was a miracle of instruction, and this one is no different.

Jerusalem is 2,500 feet above sea level. It sits on top of Mount Zion. Jericho is at the lowest spot on Earth, right on the shore of the Dead Sea, 1,400 feet below sea level. So, the picture in Christ's parable is of a man traveling down, down, down—from Jerusalem, the holy city, to Jericho, the heathen city.

This was a very treacherous route in that day and can still be today. There were limestone caves where gangs could hide, just trying to catch someone on that lonely highway, and this was no exception. So as this man was going down with his back toward the holy place and his face toward the hellish place, he was pounced upon by thieves.

THE THIEVES: SATAN

These thieves in the parable represent the devil. "The thief does not come except to steal and kill and destroy" (John 10:10a).

All around you there are people who are like these thieves. There is a hardened cruelty, a callousness in society. I am appalled to read what humans will do to other humans.

There are really three levels of life. There are those, like these thieves, who say, "What's yours is mine, and I'm going to take it from you." There are those, like the priest and Levite, who say, "What's mine is mine and I'm going to keep it." Then there are those, like the good Samaritan, who say, "It is not really mine. I'm just a steward over it, and I will share with you whatever you need, in the name of Almighty God, because I love God."

So, this man in the parable is within an inch of dying; battered, bruised, bleeding, broken, robbed, destitute by the side of the road.

THE PRIEST: RITUALISM

Along comes a priest, who looks at him, understands his condition, and goes right on.

I read of a man once who was walking down the streets of a big city and told his friends what he saw. He said, "They are so cruel and heartless in these big cities. I passed by a man asleep in a doorway. The dirt and newspapers and everything had blown around this man, and he was asleep there on the concrete. There was a piece of humanity on the ground, but people were just passing by." Then he said, "And when we came back from lunch, he was still there." Hello! We see them. We beat our breasts. "Too bad." That is what the priest did.

The priest in the parable represents ritualism. The priests were the ones who performed religious ceremonies and rituals. But Jesus is teaching here that religious ritual cannot save anybody. It never has; never will.

THE LEVITE: LEGALISM

Then a Levite came. The Levites were the keepers of the Law, the experts, the legalists of that day. We try to help society with rituals and rules, and it will never, ever get done.

The Levite may have lectured the injured man. "You should never have been out on a lonely road like this. You have been headed in the wrong direction anyway. Do you see what your disobedience has done to you? You are suffering the consequences."

The Law can describe us, but the Law cannot deliver us.

THE GOOD SAMARITAN: CHRIST

Along comes the Good Samaritan. The Samaritans were hated, despised, looked down upon as a mongrel race. The Jews sniffed at them and did not want to have company with them. So, Jesus uses this story very wisely—because the Samaritan is going to represent Jesus Christ Himself. Jesus, like that Samaritan, was despised and rejected of men. Jesus went to this man and performed an act of compassion, an act of caring.

What does your church need to be? A church of compassion. A church grows when people meet love, compassion, and friendship there—when it is a caring church. Somebody once asked a little boy why he passed so many churches on his way to one particular church. He said, "Because they love a guy over there."

Take a look at the compassion of the Lord Jesus Christ—who tells us, "Go and do likewise."

WHAT IS GENUINE COMPASSION?

This is not sentimentality. When Jesus said that this Samaritan "had pity on him," He used the strongest word for compassion that we find in the Bible. It means he was moved from the depth of his being.

Com means "with." *Passion* means "suffering." To be moved with compassion means that you literally suffer with somebody else. The priest saw and passed by. The Levite saw and passed by. But the Good Samaritan, who represents Jesus Christ, went to him.

We all have to be careful. Sometimes I get so surrounded by people that if I am not careful, my heart can get tough, and I can lose tenderness.

I was in an airport some time back, before they outlawed smoking in the airport. I had some work to do, so I found a place where there was no one around. I opened my briefcase and got out my work. There were no people around me, and plenty of places to sit.

But a man came and sat down right next to me and took out a cigarette. I was breathing into my nostrils the smoke out of that man's nose.

I did not say a word to him. I folded up my books and so forth, and I moved all the way across the hall.

That man got up and came all the way across the hall and sat down by me and lit another cigarette.

I still, by the grace of God, did not say anything (I won't tell you what I was thinking). I folded up my stuff and put it back in the briefcase.

He said, "Don't leave! Please, don't leave! Aren't you Adrian Rogers?"

"Yes, I am."

He said, "I need to talk with you. Will you, please? I'll put out the cigarette."

I talked to that man, and I thought, *how careless and callous can I be?* There are hurting people who need us.

This Good Samaritan in Jesus' parable had genuine compassion. The Bible says he "came where the man was." We sit in our stained-glass country clubs and wonder why they do not come to church.

Christians, do you find it difficult to get to church on Sunday morning? If you have children, you really do. It is harder to get to church on Sunday morning than it is to get the kids ready for school on Monday. Why? Because the devil does not want you to come on Sunday morning. By the time you leave the house, it looks like a tornado hit it. People are grouchy. On the way to church you get into an argument. This happens to those who want to come.

What about those who do not want to come? We ought to be grateful when they do. There is not one shred of Scripture that tells a lost man to come to church, but there are plenty of Scriptures that tell the Church to go to the unsaved. We ought not to be amazed that they do not come. We ought to be amazed that we do not go.

GRACIOUS, GENTLE, GENEROUS

"So he went to him and bandaged his wounds, pouring on oil and wine; and he set him on his own animal, brought him to an inn, and took care of him" (Luke 10:34).

There are a lot of people whom we might prefer to avoid, and wrap ourselves in our robes of self-righteousness, but we need *gracious* compassion. Are you not glad that Jesus came to you where you were? He found me where I was. I was not seeking Him anymore than this wounded man was seeking the Good Samaritan.

The Good Samaritan poured wine into the wounds of this man to cleanse, as an antiseptic. The wine represents the blood of Jesus.

But then he poured in oil, not only to cleanse, but also to sooth. Oil in the Bible is a symbol of the Holy Spirit of God. Real compassion brings the blood that cleanses and the Spirit that comforts.

Then the Good Samaritan bound up the man's wounds with bandages. He covered him. This broken man was bound by the tender hands of the Good Samaritan.

Then he carried him on his own donkey to where he needed to go. He brought him to the inn and said, "Take care of him. Here are the resources. If that is not enough, when I come again, I will repay you." It was gentle compassion and *generous* compassion.

Jesus is saying this: Do you want to know who your neighbor is? Your neighbor is somebody who has a need. No matter where they are, no matter what it costs, we need to be like the Lord Jesus Christ.

There is a story that comes out of World War II. Every time I think about it, it haunts me.

It took place in a Polish village. The Nazis decided they needed to eradicate the Jews in that village. They took them outside of the city and made them dig a shallow grave, then lined them up—husbands, wives, children, all of them—took a machine gun, and cut them down, and they fell into that grave. Then they smoothed the grave over.

A little boy was standing there, and for whatever reason, he was not hit by a bullet. But when everyone else fell, he fell also, pretending he had been shot. They buried him, but the soil was loose, and the grave was shallow, and there was an air pocket where he could breathe. He was covered with the blood of his mother and father and caked with dirt.

He waited a while until he did not hear any noise above ground and dug his way out of that grave: bloody, dirty, frightened, alone, and orphaned.

He went to a door and knocked. A woman came out and recognized him as a Jewish boy. She knew what the danger would be to her if she harbored him. She said, "Go away!" and shut the door.

The little boy went to another house. The same thing happened. "I'm sorry, but I can't help you. Go away!"

He went to a third house. The lady came to the door and started to say something. He said, "Wait a minute. Don't you know who I am? I am the Jesus that you say you worship."

She said, "Child, come in, come in!"

You might say, "These people alongside the road, beaten and battered and bruised, are not my responsibility."

But Jesus said, "Assuredly, I say to you, inasmuch as you did it to one of the least of these My brethren, you did it to Me" (Matthew 25:40b).

It does not always have to be as dramatic as helping a little boy who has dug himself out of a grave. But in a very practical way, here is how you can make your church a more loving church in the future.

HOW TO BECOME A COMPASSIONATE CHURCH

Church leaders, you set the tone.

Sometimes I hear preachers complaining, "Oh, these people in my church…"

I say, "How long have you been there?" They tell me. Then I say, "You're not talking about them. You're talking about you." Leadership sets the tone.

You need to be approachable. Be real. Do not be phonies.

GREET PEOPLE

Learn to greet people personally when they come into church. Do not be so self-concerned that you do not greet people personally. Shake hands warmly. Be like Jesus, the Good Samaritan, who looked on this injured man. Give everyone a look, a word, a touch.

I do not mean to drape yourself around somebody's neck, to be overly familiar. But there is no spray-on compassion. Jesus touched people—not only physically, but emotionally. It is more important to influence people than to impress them.

Do you know why we have difficulty memorizing people's names? Because we are trying to impress them. We are so concentrated on ourselves that we do not fasten our eyes, our hearts, and our minds upon these people. Church, learn to smile. Laugh. Go to the mirror and practice if you have to.

A little boy was in a revival meeting once. He felt moved to witness, so he turned to a somber-looking man who looked like he had been weaned on a dill pickle, and he said, "Sir, are you a Christian?"

The man said, "Son, I'm a deacon!"

The boy said, "Mister, it doesn't matter what you done. God will save you."

Put a welcome sign on your face. Don't look like the defensive line for a football team. "Do you mean I have to smile even when I don't feel like it?" Yep!

Jesus said,

> "Moreover, when you fast, do not be like the hypocrites, with a sad countenance. For they disfigure their faces that they may appear to men to be fasting. Assuredly, I say to you, they have their reward. But you, when you fast, anoint your head and wash your face..." (Matthew 6:16-17).

Make certain your countenance reflects what is on the inside.

WATCH FIRST IMPRESSIONS

I read somewhere that when people come to a church, in the first twelve minutes they make up their minds whether or not they like it. I cannot vouch for the exactitude of that, but I believe there is enough truth in it.

It is so important that you find a guest and do what I have said: greet them personally, put a smile on your face that says, "Welcome."

We had something happen in our church once, right down at the front—one of our members, a woman, came in, and there was a stranger, a guest, sitting in her seat.

The woman said to that guest, "You're going to have to move. That's my seat."

Can you believe that? That woman should have been willing to stand outside in the rain to let a guest sit in that seat. It is not your seat. It belongs to Jesus. We need to watch the first impressions we make.

When you fly, how do you get your impression of the airline? Not from the president of the airline, or the pilot, but from the ticket clerk and the stewardess. They are more important to you.

It is not enough to come and hear the sermon. It is not enough to hear the choir. Church members, when people walk in the door, you are the ones on the front lines to make them feel welcome—to be the good Samaritan.

We do not need to embarrass our guests. Never try to manipulate people. Let me help you to imagine what an unsaved or an unchurched person may feel when they come to a church.

Imagine that you have neighbors who are Buddhists. They invite you to a Buddhist temple. You do not want to go, but they are good neighbors, and you love them, so finally, you go. You would be frightened. You would think everybody there knows that you are not a Buddhist and that they are all watching you.

Do you know the three biggest social fears people have?

One: to go to a party with perfect strangers. Two: to make a speech in public. Three: to answer personal questions in public. And what do we do? We get guests in a Sunday school class, and we say, "Stand up and tell us something about yourself." Inside, they are dying!

Make them feel welcome with a gift of hospitality. Have name tags so that if they do not know a person's name, they can glance across and see it.

Sometimes in our church, we think we are having fellowship. We think we are so loving—but who are we loving? One another! We get into our holy huddles, our Sacred Society for Snubbing Sinners. They are around us and we do not know it.

A while back, I came out into the sanctuary early before a service. The place was about a third filled. I saw a young lady sitting by herself—maybe in her mid-twenties or thirties. I thought, *she looks a little lonely.*

I went and sat down beside her. I asked her, "How are you doing?"

She said, "Not good at all."

I said, "Well, tell me about it."

"My husband has left us. He has forsaken me and the children. I don't know what to do. Thank you for coming to sit by me." I tried to minister to her and give her a word of encouragement, and to pray for her.

I got a letter from her later. She wrote, "You will never know this side of Heaven what that meant. I was ready to throw it all in, but I said to God, 'I'm going to church one more time. God, if you really love me, let me know it.' Of all the people in that vast auditorium, you came and sat down beside me and prayed for me and cared for me."

We need to practice caring, non-judgmental love. That is

what Jesus did.

APPROVAL VS. ACCEPTANCE

We can accept people without approval.

We may not approve of the way they dress, the way they look. I will tell you: one thing I don't care for is certain body piercings. But if you are in my church with a piercing of some kind, the point is that you are very welcome. There is a difference between approval and acceptance.

Do you know why they crucified Jesus? Because they said He was a friend of sinners. This Good Samaritan went down to a man who had turned his back on Jerusalem, who was going down to Jericho. Jesus did not come to condemn; He came to save.

He never lowered the standard. The Bible says that He is, "holy, harmless, undefiled, separate from sinners, and has become higher than the heavens" (Hebrews 7:26b), yet He came to us where we are.

Rituals and rules are not enough. This world needs our compassion. If your church, especially your leadership, can learn to love and care, it is incredible what God will do through you.

Commit yourself to Jesus Christ. What a mighty army God has given us! Be faithful unto death! Be faithful! Be faithful! Be faithful!

AFTERWORD

At the conclusion of Pastor Rogers' final sermon in the series about God's charge for the Church, he spoke passionately to his specific congregation upon his retirement. These thoughts may be especially useful for church leaders during periods of transition.

These were his final, final words from the pulpit.

If Bellevue and our leadership can learn to love and to care, friend, it is incredible what God will do through this church. My prayer for Bellevue Baptist Church is that we will be a caring church. Our rituals, our rules, are not enough. This world needs our compassion.

Now, here's what we're going to do tonight. Ushers, would you stand. The ushers have a form they're going to pass one out to you tonight. On one side it says, "Our Commitment." On the other side, it speaks of Bellevue's mission statement. Now, I've asked you to memorize Bellevue's mission statement, but perhaps you've never even known we have one.

Bellevue Baptist Church exists for the purpose of: Magnifying JESUS through worship and the Word, moving believers in JESUS toward maturity and ministry, and making JESUS known to our neighbors and the nations.

That's what we're all about, and you're a part of it, and you need to acknowledge Jesus Christ as your Lord and Savior, as the Head of the church, and faithfully commit to Him and to His church.

You're not going to give it to me. It's a bookmark to put in your Bible.

These are the first three commitments:

- I commit to pray for our search committee.
- I commit to pray for my church. It's your church and His church.
- I commit to continue my leadership responsibilities.

Don't you dare say when we're without a pastor and the search committee is doing its work, that's the time for you to let down. It is not! Don't say, "Well, Adrian's not here this morning. Let's go over to ABC Church." Don't do it! If there's ever a time when you need to be faithful, this is the time to continue your leadership responsibilities.

Here are three more commitments:

- I commit to support my church staff.
- I commit to be faithful in my church attendance.
- I commit to pray for and support our new pastor.

Now, we have a wonderful staff–good and godly men and women–and they serve you, and you need to support them and pray for them.

Regarding your attendance, I'm grateful you're here tonight. It's a rainy night, but I don't really brag on you too much for that when early Christians faced the lions and the flame and beating and stoning for the privilege of worshiping together.

Now, church, listen to me. We have a committee. We prayerfully selected that committee. We have been praying for that committee day after day after day. I hope you have. So, we're praying and asking God and believing God.

We have a committee, a God-anointed and God-appointed committee, if we're praying for them, whoever they recommend to us, we're going to say amen. I would not think of refusing to approve someone that this committee presents to us. I wouldn't even think about it. Why? Because I believe they're God's people. We have prayed. We have believed God. Nobody is going to please everybody. If he does, he'll please the devil most of all. Every now and then, people say, "Oh pastor, everybody loves you." I say, "Hardity har-har-har." No, they don't! But this church, and especially our core leadership, supports the present pastor and will support the new one.

Here's the final commitment:

- I promise to honor God in all my words and actions. I will never do anything to disgrace the name of Jesus or His Church.

I'm going to ask you to make this commitment and to sign this and put it in your Bible.

COMMITMENT PRAYER AND FINAL CHARGE

At this point, Pastor Rogers asked all those in the church in leadership to come down to the front of the worship center. This included the associate pastor, the lay executive committee of three who would support the associate pastor, the church's executive staff, all ordained ministers in the church, all deacon officers, all church staff, all members of the pastor search committee, all church committee chairpersons, all teachers of Bible Fellowship classes from children through adults and all choir officers.

Once those in leadership had assembled, Pastor Rogers prayed for them and for the entire congregation. He also gave this final, final charge:

> Now, let me say a word to all of you. The Bible says, "Be ye clean that bear the vessels of the Lord." I would be absolutely petrified to serve in any position represented here with an unclean heart. There's no excuse for one. If you have anything in your heart toward another person that's not right, any ungodly habit, anything that anyone has anything against you that you've not tried to make right, I admonish you, I challenge you in the name of Jesus to make it right. I want you, friends, to be as pure as the driven snow, to be as holy as God can make a man or a woman, I want you to be that way. These are serious days. Even if we were not getting a new pastor, these are serious days. And I want you, please, for Jesus' sake and our sake, to be all that you can be.
>
> One of the proverbs that I use frequently—it's not a Bible proverb, but it is certainly a proverb that stirs my heart—it asks a question. Here's the question. If the gold rusts, what shall the iron do? You're supposed to be the gold. I mean, you're the leaders. The Bible says of a pastor, he's to be a man found blameless. We're not sinless, but we're to be blameless. Nobody can point the finger of blame at us and

AFTERWORD

say, "It is your fault." I want you to double and redouble your faithfulness. Do not let down in this period of time. Do not get discouraged. Believe God. And do better, by God's grace, than you've ever done.

And what I'm saying to these dear people out here or up here, I'm saying to you folks out there. We're going to commit ourselves and recommit ourselves to Jesus Christ tonight. What a mighty army God has given us. I'm so grateful for each of you. I love you, I salute you, and I'll never stop loving you till Jesus comes. Be faithful unto death! Be faithful! Be faithful! Be faithful! In the name of Jesus!

SPECIAL NOTE

Should you desire to share this with your small group or your congregation, this content is also available in the eight-week Bible study, "God's Plan for the Church," available at lwf.org. *

Special discount for groups or churches

WILL YOU SUPPORT LOVE WORTH FINDING?

This ministry is funded primarily by gifts from Christians committed to sharing God's Word with lost and hurting people from all walks of life.

———

If this resource has been a help to you, please consider joining with us to bless others with the Gospel of Jesus Christ.

lwf.org/give

Or call 800-274-5683

For additional copies of this book or to browse other available resources, visit **lwf.org**.

www.ingramcontent.com/pod-product-compliance
Lightning Source LLC
Chambersburg PA
CBHW051952290426
44110CB00015B/2209